SHAPING SHAWLS

Shaping Shawls
shawl construction & 10 designs
Anna Dalvi

Cooperative Press
Cleveland, Ohio

Library of Congress Control Number: 2011932481
ISBN 13: 978-0-9792017-6-9
First Edition
Published by Cooperative Press
www.cooperativepress.com

Text and patterns © 2011, Anna Dalvi
Photography © 2011, Kristen Caldwell for Kristen Caldwell Photography LLC
Illustrations © 2011, MJ Kim
Page motif decorations © 2011, Terry Cutlip for Sassy Designs, Inc
Photographic backdrops by Bad Sass Backdrops, Inc
All rights reserved.

Makeup artist: Elle Gemma for Spell Cosmetics
Models: Arabella Proffer, Elle Gemma, Maria Miranda, Michelle Muldrow

Cooperative Press
Senior Editor: Shannon Okey
Technical Editor: Andrea Smith

Visit Anna Dalvi's website at http://www.knitandknag.com
Visit Cooperative Press at http://www.cooperativepress.com

To Aneesh
without whom this book never would have been written,
and to Linnéa, Axel and Viggo
my biggest fans and greatest supporters.

Table of Contents:
Shaping Shawls

Chapter ONE 9
Introduction and lace design basics

WHEN NUMBERS DON'T STAY THE SAME. 11
BLOCKING. 12
STOCKINETTE VS. GARTER BASED SHAWLS. 13
GAUGE & YARN WEIGHT. 13
TOOLS FOR DESIGNING 14
CAST ON TECHNIQUES 15
BIND OFF TECHNIQUES 16

Chapter TWO 19
Rectangular shawls, no edging
Perilla 20

Chapter THREE 25
Triangular shawls, bottom up
Margarita Leaves 27

Chapter FOUR 33
Triangular shawls, neck to edge
Magic Lanterns 33

Chapter FIVE 41
Creating additional canvas space on triangular shawls for visual interest
Mystic Roses 42

Chapter SIX 53
Variations on triangular shawls
Tidal Waves 54

Changing Directions 57

Chandelier Shawl 67

Chapter SEVEN 75
Edging on rectangular shawls (knit with shawl)
Blueberry Patch 76

Chapter EIGHT 83
Square shawls
Araneidae 84

Mystic Air 89

Abbreviations 102

Stitch Legend 103

Recommended Books 104

Acknowledgements 105

About Anna Dalvi 106

About Cooperative Press 107

Also by Cooperative Press 107

Sample Charts 108

Chapter ONE:
Introduction and Lace Design Basics

I love to knit lace, because it is so interesting to watch the patterns develop on my needles. Simple yarn overs and decreases combine into amazing patterns that look so complex; and yet, when broken down to the most basic elements, lace patterns are nothing but a combination of knits, purls, yarn overs and decreases. That's all!

I've written this book to share some of the things that I have learned over the years while designing lace. When I decided to design my first lace shawl, I had to sit down and figure out how to build a triangle. I thought I would cast on a couple of stitches that would form the bottom point and work up towards the top. It seemed to work well, and I was very pleased with the result. But then I noticed that a lot of the triangular lace shawls already out there were knit from the top down and consisted of two triangles. So I tried that construction, and figured out a formula for shaping it. Once I had done that, I wanted to elaborate on the design, so I added lace panels down the spine and along the edges. And so it continued...

Every lace shawl I have designed has been an exploration in shapes, and I have made multiple variations on the main shapes. As with anything, lace design can be done in many different ways, and it is this difference between us that make our shawls unique. I would like to share some of the building blocks I use with you, in the hopes that you will take them and use them to create new and interesting combinations. I've attempted to cover the various shapes and constructions in the same order that I "discovered" them — from simple to more advanced.

Lace is no more difficult to knit than anything else, provided you take it one stitch at a time. However, when designing lace shawls there are a few things to keep in mind that will help keep you on track. The two main things to consider are the overall shaping of the shawl and the area which you will fill up with a lace pattern or patterns — the *canvas* of the shawl.

If you consider your shawl a canvas that needs to be filled with lace designs, then the shawl shaping will determine the shape and size of the canvas you have to play with. There are nearly endless options when it comes to shaping your shawl, but the most basic ones are rectangular shawls (stoles/scarves), triangular shawls, and square shawls. All of these shapes are covered in this book, along with a number of variations. In this book, I have opted not to cover circular or semi-circular shawls, as their construction is not based on triangles or straight lines.

Once the shape is determined, and the construction decided, a designer can fill his or her canvas with all sorts of amazing designs and stitch combinations. And aside from the shaping of the shawl, the stitch count should stay constant on each row (for exceptions to this rule, see "When Numbers DON'T Stay The Same" on page 11). Expressed in the most basic way, this means that for each increase, there must be a matching decrease.

In mathematical terms, difference can be expressed as a *delta*. In this instance, the delta is the difference between how many stitches were used from the previous row, and how many stitches were created for the next row.

```
-[stitches used] + [stitches created] = delta
```

STITCH	DELTA	REASON
k1	0	uses one stitch from the previous row to create one stitch for the next row -1 + 1 = 0
p1	0	uses one stitch from the previous row to create one stitch for the next row -1 + 1 = 0
yo	1	uses no stitches from the previous row, but creates one stitch for the next row 0 + 1 = 1
ssk	-1	uses two stitches from the previous row to create one stitch for the next row -2 + 1 = -1
k2tog	-1	uses two stitches from the previous row to create one stitch for the next row -2 + 1 = -1
ssp	-1	uses two stitches from the previous row to create one stitch for the next row -2 + 1 = -1
p2tog	-1	uses two stitches from the previous row to create one stitch for the next row -2 + 1 = -1
k3tog	-2	uses three stitches from the previous row to create one stitch for the next row -3 + 1 = -2
sl1-k2tog-psso	-2	uses three stitches from the previous row to create one stitch for the next row -3 + 1 = -2
sl2-k-psso	-2	uses three stitches from the previous row to create one stitch for the next row -3 + 1 = -2

There are many special stitches available to the creative knitter, but they can all be analyzed to see how they affect the stitch count in the row. For example, some Estonian lace motifs include stitches like "make 3 from 5". They use five stitches from the previous row and turn them into three stitches on the current row.

$$-5 + 3 = -2$$

This means that this particular stitch reduces the stitch count in the row by 2. The sum of all the deltas for each stitch on the row should yield 0 if the stitch count is to stay constant.

Calculating the delta for each row while designing a lace shawl can help find mistakes in the patterns. Generally, in order for the stitch count to stay the same, each increase must have a matching decrease. But sometimes the designer can make mistakes while charting patterns, and the stitch count is not correct for the next row. If the stitch count keeps changing erratically from row to row, this will affect the shape of the finished shawl. Instead of the rectangular shawl you were hoping for, your edges may not be straight at all!

For an example of how the delta can be applied, consider the simple Cat's Paw lace pattern.

In written form, the pattern looks like this:

Row 1: K9
Row 3: K2, k2tog, yo, k, yo, ssk, k2
Row 5: K, k2tog, yo, k3, yo, ssk, k
Row 7: K3, k2tog, yo, k3, yo, ssk, k
Row 9: K9

To calculate the delta for row 1, substitute each stitch with its associated delta. For k, the delta is 0, which means that for row 1 the delta = 0*9 = 0

To calculate the delta for Row 3, substitute each stitch with its associated delta like this:

k2	k2tog	yo	k	yo	ssk	k2
2*0	-1	1	0	1	-1	2*0

Then add up the deltas in the table to get a total sum of 0. This means that at the end of row 3 we have the same number of stitches as we did at the end of row 1. Calculate the delta for Row 5 in the same way:

k	k2tog	yo	k3	yo	ssk	k
0	-1	1	3*0	1	-1	0

Adding up the deltas for each stitch, we find that the delta for row 5 is also 0. The same holds true for row 7 and row 9, which means that the entire lace pattern is balanced, and will be a good choice to use in decorating the canvas of your shawl. Generally there is no need to calculate the delta for each row when knitting from a purchased pattern, as you can assume that the pattern has been both tested and edited. However, we all know that errors occasionally slip through, even for the most thorough designers. So if you ever find that you have too many or too few stitches on your needles while following a pattern, calculating the delta can help you determine if there is a problem with the pattern, or with your knitting. If you don't have as many stitches on your needles as the pattern specifies, there is most likely a problem with the knitting. If you have as many stitches on your needles as the pattern calls for, but it still doesn't work out, there may well be a problem with the pattern, and you should check for errata.

WHEN NUMBERS DON'T STAY THE SAME

As with everything, there are exceptions when it comes to lace design. There are many lace patterns where the stitch count does NOT stay constant from row to row in the motif. But since lace fabric is flexible, it can still be blocked into the desired shape, assuming the stitch count doesn't change too drastically. (There is no numerical definition of "too drastically," it is simply a judgement call). For example, in the following chart, the stitch count is not constant from row to row:

The pattern would start by casting on 31 stitches. To calculate the delta for row 1, first convert the chart to written instructions. Row 1 (as read from right to left):

K2, yo, k2tog, k2, k2tog, yo, k, yo, ssk, k3, 3x3, k3, k2tog, yo, k, yo, ssk, k2, ssk, yo, k2

Then substitute each stitch with the correct delta, like this:

k2	yo	k2tog	k2	k2tog	yo	k	yo	ssk	k3	3x3	k3	k2tog
2*0	1	-1	2*0	-1	1	0	1	-1	3*0	0	3*0	-1
yo	k	yo	ssk	k2	ssk	yo	k2					
1	0	1	-1	2*0	-1	1	2*0					

Finally, add up the deltas for each stitch to get the total delta for the row. In this case, the sum is 0, which means that at the end of the row, the stitch count has stayed constant. That is to say that at the end of row 1 you have the same number of stitches you started with. Row 3:

K2, yo, k2tog, k, k2tog, yo, k3, yo, ssk, k2tog, yo, k, yo, k, yo, k, yo, ssk, k2tog, yo, k3, yo, ssk, k, ssk, yo, k2

Then substitute each stitch with the correct delta, like this:

k2	yo	k2tog	k	k2tog	yo	k3	yo	ssk	k2tog	yo	k	yo
2*0	1	-1	0	-1	1	3*0	1	-1	-1	1	0	1
k	yo	k	yo	ssk	k2tog	yo	k3	yo	ssk	k	ssk	yo
0	1	0	1	-1	-1	1	3*0	1	-1	0	-1	1
k2												
2*0												

Add up the deltas for each stitch to get the total delta for the row. In this case, the sum is 2, which means that at the end of row 3, the stitch count is 2 stitches greater than at the end of row 1. If you consider the chart, you will see that this comes from the two unmatched yarn-overs near the center of the row. Row 5:

K2, yo, k2tog, k2tog, yo, k5, yo, ssk, k2tog, yo, sl2-k-psso, yo, ssk, k2tog, yo, k5, yo, ssk, ssk, yo, k2

Then substitute each stitch with the correct delta, like this:

k2	yo	k2tog	k2tog	yo	k5	yo	ssk	k2tog	yo	⋀	yo	ssk
2*0	1	-1	-1	1	5*0	1	-1	-1	1	-2	1	-1
k2tog	yo	k5	yo	ssk	ssk	yo	k2					
-1	1	5*0	1	-1	-1	1	2*0					

And add up the deltas for each stitch to get the total delta for the row. For row 5 the delta is -2. That means that at the end of row 5 the stitch count is 2 stitches less than at the end of row 3. And that, in turn, means that we are back to the same stitch count as we were at the end of row 1.

The delta for row 7 is also 0. And the delta for row 9 is 4. This means that at the end of row 9, we have four extra stitches on the needles. But then row 11 has a delta of -4, which brings us back to the same stitch count as for rows 1, 5 and 7. So on the whole, while the stitch count varies, it does so in a controlled way, and is generally brought back to 31.

For the purposes of explaining shaping in this book, I have chosen to assume that the stitch count always stays constant within the canvas of the shawl. As you get more adept at designing lace patterns, feel free to experiment with this "rule".

BLOCKING

In addition to the shaping and the stitch count, there are a few basics to consider when designing a lace shawl. Lace motifs always look better when blocked, so plan on blocking your finished shawl. This will stretch the fabric and make the knitting look more even and opens up the lace motifs. The yarn needs to adjust to being in a new shape after spending who knows how long rolled up into a ball. As the yarn is knit, it's still not adjusted to being turned into stitches and tends to fight its new shape. This means that the fabric of the shawl looks lumpy and the holes aren't very well defined. Here, the unblocked, in-progress shawl is on the left, and a closeup of the same shawl's fabric, blocked, is on the right.

When the shawl is finished, and all ends are sewn in, soak the shawl in water and then pin it out to block. Leave it pinned out until the shawl is completely dry, and you will see an astonishing transformation. The yarn has now settled into its new shape, and the yarn-overs and other stitches are more well-defined. In the unblocked version, it was difficult to tell what the motifs looked like, but in the blocked version the motifs are very clear.

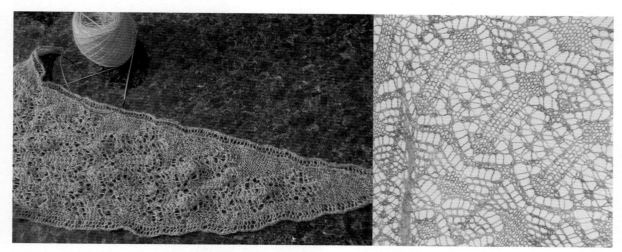

STOCKINETTE VS. GARTER BASED SHAWLS

If your shawl is stockinette-based, be aware that stockinette-based knitting has a tendency to curl. You can block it flat, but once it is released from the blocking board, the edges will curl up. To avoid this, it is important that you factor in some edge stitches to the design in order to stabilize the shawl and prevent curling. Garter stitch at the beginning and end of each row is the most common solution. The patterns in this book use a few different edge stitch variations, but there are lots of other possibilities that you can use when designing your own shawl. Experiment and find the ones you like best.

GAUGE & YARN WEIGHT

For a shawl, gauge is not as critical as it is for a sweater — that is to say, if your shawl is somewhat larger or smaller than mine, it doesn't matter.

Lace can be knit using any weight of yarn. Lace- and cobweb-weight yarn result in delicate, wispy shawls. Fingering weight yarn is my personal favorite for everyday wear shawls, as they give a little bit more weight to the shawl and I'm not as worried about snagging their intricate lace on zippers and buttons. Heavier yarns can be used for warmer winter shawls.

To determine the best combination of yarn and needles, you need to swatch. Knit a swatch and make sure you like the texture and appearance of the fabric you've created. The important thing to look for in a lace swatch is the difference between the yarn overs (the holes) and the knits (the solid part). There is no right and wrong, just personal preference.

This is also the appropriate time to consider fabric drape. If you find that the fabric in your swatch is too stiff, you can go up a needle size or two. If the fabric is too loose and the holes are too big, you can go down in needle size.

Different yarns will also create different types of fabric depending on their fiber content. For example, a 100% silk yarn in lace-weight tends to create a shiny shawl that's very thin and wispy, whereas a 100% merino lace-weight yarn tends to have a bit more "body" and heft to it. Once you're happy with your swatch's fabric, measure its size. These measurements can be used to estimate the final width and length of your shawl. (In the case of many shawl patterns, you can simply keep knitting until you reach the desired size, then bind off). Next, choose your shawl's shape — which gives you your canvas — and appropriate edge stitches. Now it's time to start filling up that canvas with beautiful lace!

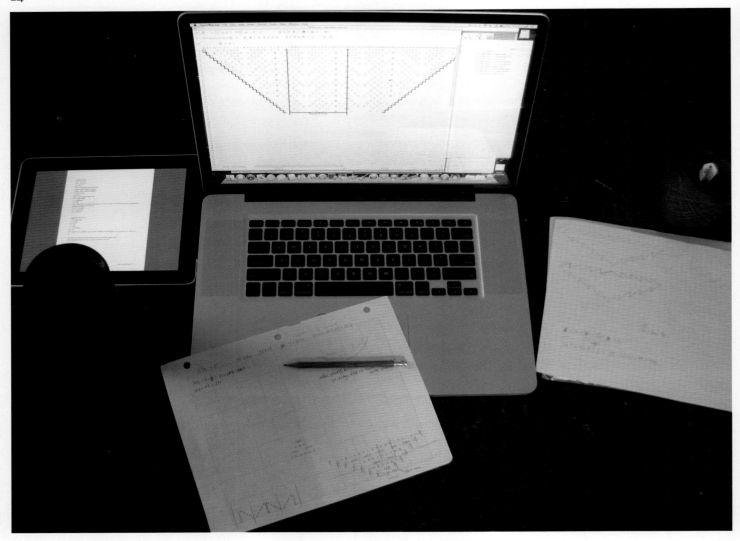

TOOLS FOR DESIGNING

Everyone plans their designs slightly differently and uses slightly different tools, but here are some that I use a lot. First of all, I find that graph paper and a pencil are essential tools. I plan all my designs in chart form, and I like to start planning the placement of the lace patterns on paper. I can either use plain graph paper, or I often start with the sample charts included in this book (pages 108-109). That way I don't have to draw a triangle outline (for a triangular shawl), but can begin placing the lace motifs right away.

I also chart things on the computer. There are lots of fancy computer programs, such as InDesign or KnitVisualizer, and they can help when charting. But it is quite possible to chart designs in Excel, or in any similar spreadsheet program. Installing a real knitting font on your computer helps immensely. There are many available: we used Aire River[1] in this book and its charts. Since I like to swatch and try out new stitch patterns and combinations, needles and yarn are essentials for me, as with any knitting designer (surprise).

Aside from that, there are lots of stitch dictionaries available to aid in picking out wonderful lace patterns to use on your shawl's canvas, several of which are listed in an appendix on page 104. And of course, in addition to using existing lace motifs, it is always possible to create your own!

When placing lace motifs on your canvas, there are different strategies. In general, it can be helpful to count the number of stitches across which the pattern repeats, and if you would like to transition into a different lace motif, it flows very nicely if the new lace motif has the same stitch count for the repeats.

---

1   http://home.earthlink.net/~ardesign/knitfont.htm

Another option would be to place the lace motifs where desired, and separate them with plain stockinette/garter stitch knitting. The important thing to consider in those cases is the space between the lace motifs — negative space. Sometimes the negative space can create very strange shapes that distract from the lace pattern on the finished shawl, as the eye is often drawn to solid areas. On the other hand, the negative space can also be used as part of the pattern, when the solid blocks create geometrical shapes like diamonds, or complete pictures.

The Mystic Star[2] pattern, which is available on my website, uses negative space to create a star pattern in solid stockinette, in addition to the stars created by the lace (holes). It is shown here in greyscale to make it easier to determine how the negative space is used.

CAST ON TECHNIQUES

There are three different cast-on techniques used in the book; cabled cast-on, provisional cast-on and invisible loop cast on. The cabled cast-on is one of my favorites for lace, because it is a very stretchy cast-on. Since it is essential to block lace, the fabric tends to stretch a lot while blocking. If the cast-on isn't stretchy, the shawl can pucker in the cast-on area, and that does not look very nice.

Provisional cast-ons are used when you do not want a cast-on edge on the shawl. In this book, there are two designs using provisional cast-ons. One is Blueberry Patch (page 76) where the bottom border is knit first, and then the cast-on edge is picked up and becomes the start of the right border. That shawl has no cast-on or bound off edge, and as such, the edges are very stretchy. The second design using a provisional cast-on is Mystic Air (page 89), where the stitches are later picked up and the shawl construction changes from knitting flat to knitting in the round.

A third way in which a provisional cast-on can be used is for a stole, when the knitter can start in the center and knit towards the end of the stole, and then pick up the stitches and knit the other half.

Finally, the invisible loop cast-on is a circular cast-on in which the center loop can be pulled tight after a few rounds have been knit. It is the neatest circular cast-on I have ever encountered, but any circular cast-on would work for the shawls knit in the round.

If you wish to explore different kinds of cast-ons, there is a wealth of information available on the internet. One site that I reference often is the TECHknitting™ site[3] which describes a number of different types of cast-ons, as well as a number of other handy techniques and tricks. Another site with a number of useful videos is KnittingHelp[4], or you can just search on YouTube.

BIND OFF TECHNIQUES

Similar to the cast-on edge, it is important that the bind-off edge is very stretchy when knitting lace. For the bind-off, I favor the lace bind-off, which is worked as follows:

K2, *return sts to left needle, k2tog through back loop, k1, repeat from * until no unworked stitches remain.

This creates a very flexible and stretchy bound off edge, and the lace fabric will not pucker around the edge.

Let's start shaping shawls!

at right: Mystic Roses, page 42

---

3   http://techknitting.blogspot.com
4   http://knittinghelp.com

Chapter TWO:
Rectangular shawls, no edging

When we all learned how to knit, we were told to cast on some stitches, and just keep knitting — no increases and no decreases — until we reached some reasonable length to bind off. A basic rectangular scarf or stole is exactly that — there is no shaping required.

To create your own rectangular shawl, first determine how wide you would like your shawl and that, along with your gauge, will give you an approximate number of stitches to cast on. A rectangular shawl can be created by casting on for the width of the rectangle and adding length by knitting more rows. OR it can be created by casting on for the length of the rectangle, and adding width by knitting more rows. Either way, you are creating a rectangle. The construction method is exactly the same.

In order to make it a little bit more interesting than that very first garter-stitch scarf we made, we can decorate the main canvas with lace patterns.

The next thing to decide is whether you want to use garter-based lace or stockinette based lace. In general, most of the simple lace motifs have lace patterning (yarn-overs and decreases) on every other row — the right-side row. And the other row (wrong-side or return row) is either purled, for stockinette based lace, or knit for garter-based lace.

If you decide to make a garter-based lace scarf, you can go ahead and start placing the lace motifs on your canvas. However, as stockinette-based knitting of any kind (including lace) has a tendency to curl at the edges, you have to plan to include some kind of stabilizing edge stitches so that the scarf does not curl. The absolute easiest way is to start the scarf off with a few plain knit rows, and then, when you get to the lace section, have a few stitches at the beginning and the end of the row in garter stitch. This means that the first and last 2-4 stitches will be knit on every row, including the return rows. For example:

Row 1: K
Row 2: K
Row 3: K3, pattern to last 3 sts, k3
Row 4: as row 3

Remember, as the shawl is knit, the stitch count has to stay the same on each row. This means that all increases in the lace motifs must have matching decreases, so count the number of stitches that you cast on at the beginning. At the beginning and end of every row of the scarf/stole, you should have the same number of stitches on your needles. If you do not, there is an unmatched yarn-over or decrease somewhere on that row. (Refer back to page 11 for exceptions to the rule).

Now, back to the number of stitches to cast on. When you decide what sort of lace patterning to use on your main canvas, try to adjust the number of stitches to cast on so that you can use whole pattern repeats.

If you have decided that you would like your stole to be approximately 70 stitches wide, and you pick a lace pattern where the pattern-repeat is 9 stitches wide, you will have to make some adjustments.

First determine how many stitches you need for your edging. Let's assume that you want 4 garter stitches at the beginning and the end of the row. That means that a total of 8 stitches are used for the edging. $8 + 9*X$ cannot equal 70 stitches if X is a whole number, since 70-8=62 and 62 is not a multiple of 9. However, $7*9=63$, which is very close to 62. So if you cast on $8 + 9*7 = 71$ stitches instead, you will end up with a scarf that has seven repeats of the lace pattern and 4 border stitches on either side, *and* a 71-stitch scarf will not be noticeably wider than a 70-stitch scarf.

In this example, each row of the pattern can be expressed as:

K4, [9 st patt rep] 7 times, k4

A handy trick when setting up the lace pattern on your needles is to use stitch-markers to mark every pattern repeat, as well as separating the border stitches from the canvas of the shawl. In the example above, you could place a stitch marker after 4 stitches, separating the garter stitch from the lace pattern, and then every 9 stitches. The last stitch-marker would end up 4 stitches from the end of the row, separating the last pattern-repeat from the left-side garter stitch.

Another good idea is to use a lifeline every so often, in case you make a mistake and need to rip back your work. There is no hard and fast rule on how often to add a lifeline — many knitters live dangerously and never use them — but as a rule of thumb consider how far you would be willing to rip back in case things went wrong, and add lifelines as appropriate.

Perilla

The Perilla scarf a is a rectangular scarf/stole that is worked from two ends and grafted together in the center. The patterning on the scarf is built from a number of 12-stitch repeats. This makes the width of the scarf easily adjustable so that the knitter can make anything from a thin scarf to a wide stole using the same pattern. It also allows the knitter more flexibility in choosing the yarn, because anything from a thin lace-weight to super bulky yarn could be used.

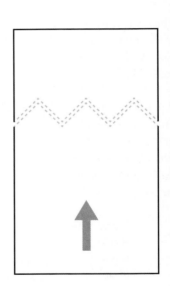

Since it is a stockinette based pattern, it is important to include some stabilizing edge stitches so that the scarf does not curl. In this case, I have opted for 4 stitches at the beginning and the end of the rows that are worked in garter-stitch lace.

The cast-on edge is done with an Estonian technique of knitting on the stitches with a double strand of yarn. One strand is then cut off, leaving enough length to weave in the ends and the knitting continues with one strand only. This makes the cast-on edge a little thicker than the other rows, and gives it a little bit more definition than a single-stranded cast-on. Since it is a very distinctive look, this scarf is worked from two ends so that both ends of the scarf will look identical.

The scarf is not grafted in the center, but rather closer to one side than the other. The cast-on and the initial edging pattern is worked the same way on both ends, but the main pattern on the scarf is worked from one end to the other. This way the pattern flows nicely through the length of the scarf, and the grafting is hidden where the pattern changes from the diamond pattern to the edging (row 30).

The Perilla Scarf is inspired by the Perilla mint plant. Mint comes in many different forms, and was originally brought to North America by Asian immigrants. The plant spread quickly and can now be found in sunny, open fields, along roads and in wooded areas. The purple leaves of the Perilla plant are a decorative addition to any garden.

MATERIALS

1 skein SweetGeorgia Yarns CashSilk Lace [45% cashmere, 55% silk; 400yds per 50g skein] shown in Boysenberry
1 set US 6 [4mm] needles
Large-eyed, blunt needle

GAUGE

18 sts and 20 rows = 4 in [10 cm] in pattern, blocked

FINISHED (BLOCKED) SIZE

Width: 10 inches [26 cm] with 3 repeats
Length: 72 inches [194 cm] adjustable in pattern

INSTRUCTIONS

This scarf can be made wider by adding repeats of the 12 st pattern in the center

PIECE A

CO 45 sts (plus any multiple of 12 if you desire a wider scarf/stole) using a cabled cast-on with double strand of yarn
Cut off one of the strands of yarn leaving enough length to weave in later. Continue knitting with one strand of yarn only.
Knit 2 rows, then begin chart as follows:
Work rows 1-29, then put aside on a stitch-holder. This is your top-edging, and will be grafted to piece B to finish the scarf.

PIECE B

CO the same number of stitches as before using a cabled cast-on with double strand of yarn
Cut off one of the strands of yarn leaving enough length to weave in later. Continue knitting with one strand of yarn only.
Knit 2 rows, then continue with the chart. Work rows 1-54.
Repeat rows 31-54 as many times as necessary to reach the desired length of the scarf minus the length of piece A, and then work rows 31-35.
Then graft the two pieces of the scarf together using kitchener stitch.
Sew in ends and block.

DELTA ANALYSIS

To analyze the chart in the Perilla Scarf, start with the number of stitches cast on. In the case of knitting the chart as written, with no additional repeats of the center section, there are 45 stitches on the starting row. Each of the stitches used in the pattern have an associated delta.

```
k = 0
p = 0
ssk = -1
k2tog = -1
sl2-k1-psso = -2
yo = 1
```

The special stitch 3x3 uses three stitches to make three stitches, which means that the delta is 0.

```
3x3 = 0
```

To calculate the delta for row 1, first convert the chart to written instructions:

Row 1 (as read from right to left):

```
yo, k2tog, yo, k2tog, ssk, k4, yo, k, yo, k4, sl2-k-psso, k4, yo, k, yo, k4, sl2-k-psso, k4, yo, k,
yo, k4, k2tog, k2tog, yo, k2
```

Then substitute each stitch with the correct delta , like this:

yo	k2tog	yo	k2tog	ssk	k4	yo	k	yo	k4	Λ	k4	yo
1	-1	1	-1	-1	4*0	1	0	1	4*0	-2	4*0	1
k	yo	k4	Λ	k4	yo	k	yo	k4	k2tog	k2tog	yo	k2
0	1	4*0	-2	4*0	1	0	1	4*0	-1	-1	1	2*0

Note: Λ represents sl2-k-psso in the charts on this page.

And finally add up the deltas for each stitch to get the total delta for the row. In this case, the sum is 0, which means that at the end of the row, the stitch count has stayed constant. That is to say that at the end of row 1 you have the same number of stitches you started with.

Row 2 (as read from left to right):

   yo, k2tog, k2, p37, k4

Then substitute each stitch with the correct delta , like this:

yo	k2tog	k2	p37	k4
1	-1	2*0	37*0	4*0

Add up the deltas for each stitch to get the total delta for the row. In this case, the sum is 0, which means that at the end of the row, the stitch count has stayed constant. That is to say that at the end of row 2 you have the same number of stitches you started with.

Row 3 (as read from right to left):

   yo, k2tog, yo, k2tog, ssk, k3, yo, k3, yo, k3, sl2-k-psso, k3, yo, k3, yo, k3, sl2-k-psso, k3, yo,
   k3, yo, k3, k2tog, k2tog, yo, k2

Then substitute each stitch with the correct delta , like this:

yo	k2tog	yo	k2tog	ssk	k3	yo	k3	yo	k3	Λ	k3	yo
1	-1	1	-1	-1	3*0	1	3*0	1	3*0	-2	3*0	1
k3	yo	k3	Λ	k3	yo	k3	yo	k3	k2tog	k2tog	yo	k2
3*0	1	3*0	-2	3*0	1	3*0	1	3*0	-1	-1	1	2*0

Add up the deltas for each stitch to get the total delta for the row. In this case, the sum is 0, which means that at the end of the row, the stitch count has stayed constant. That is to say, at the end of row 3 you have the same number of stitches you started with at the beginning. For each row on the chart of a rectangular scarf/stole, you will find that the delta is 0.

Up until now, we have covered how to knit lace in a rectangular space. The rectangles can be scarves or stoles, or even lace inserts in sweaters, if you wish. The rectangles can be knit either from short end to short end, or from long end to long end, depending on the number of stitches cast on. For scarves and stoles, they can also start in the center (with a provisional cast-on) and be worked towards the end, or start at two ends and graft the pieces together, as in Perilla. All in all, a solid ground to stand on when moving on to adding shaping to our lace!

CHART A

Row numbers (right side, bottom to top): 1, 2, 3, 4, 5, 6, 7, 8, 9, 10, 11, 12, 13, 14, 15, 16, 17, 18, 19, 20, 21, 22, 23, 24, 25, 26, 27, 28, 29, 30, 31, 32, 33, 34, 35, 36, 37, 38, 39, 40, 41, 42, 43, 44, 45, 46, 47, 48, 49, 50, 51, 52, 53, 54

Chapter THREE:
Triangular shawls, bottom up

Now that we have mastered a straight rectangular shawl, let's move on to something with a little bit of shaping. The simple triangle is a great building block, and once we know how to create a triangle, we can use that knowledge to create a number of other shapes, including more complex triangles, squares, and edgings.

The most basic triangle is created by starting at the bottom point of the triangle and working up towards the wide edge. The orientation of the lace motifs on the shawl when worn is the same as when knit.

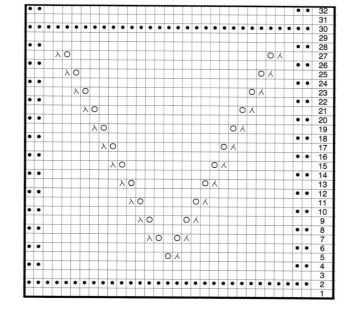

SWATCH 1

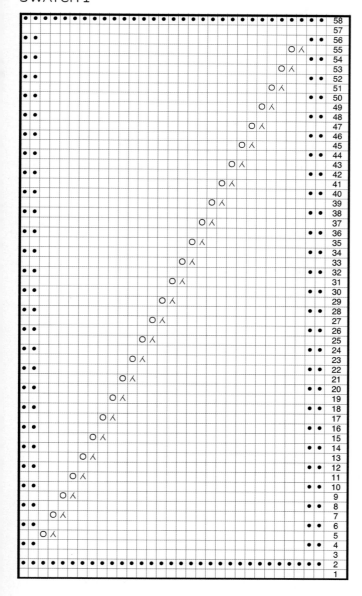

So the first thing is to figure out how to make a triangle. If you look at Swatch 1, you will see a line of yarn-overs leaning towards the right at a 45 degree angle. This line is created by shifting the yarn-overs one stitch to the left on each right-side row.

Swatch 2 shows a V of yarn-overs leaning towards the outside at a 45 degree angle. The V looks like the bottom edges of a triangular shawl. Therefore, in order to create a triangular shawl from the bottom-up, start with a small number of stitches and grow each row with one stitch near the beginning of each right-side row, and one stitch near the end of each right-side row.

SWATCH 2

The bottom-up triangle can be made to any size, and in fact, you need not determine the finished size ahead of time. You can just keep knitting and increasing one stitch near the beginning and one stitch near the end of each right-side row until you reach the desired size of shawl (or run out of yarn — whichever comes first).

Alternatively, it is also possible to start at the top edge of the shawl and cast on a large number of stitches and then decrease one stitch at the beginning and one stitch at the end of each right-side row until you are left with only one or two stitches on the needles. The motif would then be knit upside down, but the concept is the same as for a bottom-up shawl. The disadvantage of constructing a shawl in this fashion is that you must determine the finished size ahead of time, and you must cast on hundreds of stitches (and count, and count again to make sure you got the right number of stitches). There are ways to mitigate the counting problem when casting on large numbers of stitches. I like to use stitch-markers every 50 stitches, so that I only have to check the 50 stitches between each set of markers, to make sure I have the correct number of stitches cast on. It's still a lot of counting compared to the bottom-up construction. Also, if you run out of yarn before you reach the tip of the triangle, you will be out of luck, since your triangle would then be without a point (or "pointless", as it were).

The following set-up instructions can be used to create a shawl with a sharp point:

CO 2 sts
Set-up row 1 (WS): k2
Set-up row 2 (RS): kfb, kfb
Set-up row 3 (WS): k4
After the set-up instructions, proceed with charting the design.

To shape the shawl as a triangle, increase the stitch count with 2 on each right-side row. You can use any type of increase, and which one you choose is ultimately up to you as the designer. But for lace patterns, the most common way to achieve this is to use a YO near the beginning of the row and a YO near the end of the row, without matching decreases.

In the sample chart (page 109), only right side rows are charted. Wrong side rows are all k2, purl to last 2 sts, k2. This gives the shawl a garter-stitch edging, two stitches wide on each side of the shawl. The center stitch is highlighted in order to aid in centering the motif.
The canvas is growing with two stitches on each right-side row. Aside from the unmatched yarn overs on the chart, each increase in the lace patterning must have a matching decrease.

Margarita Leaves

Margarita Leaves is a bottom-up triangular lace shawl. The lace pattern consists of two main motifs — along the edges there is a diamond pattern to frame the central part of the canvas which is filled with undulating leaves.

The pattern has some lace patterning on the WS-rows, so each row is charted.

Unlike the Perilla Scarf the two lace motifs are not the same width, and they do not grow one from another. Instead, there is a clear separation between the outer frame and the central canvas. There is, however, a relationship between the size and placement of the two lace motifs. The diamonds are stacked along the sides at the same row differential (16 rows) as the height of each leaf (16 rows), and the width of the diamonds (16 sts) is twice the width of the leaves (8 sts). This makes it easy for the knitter to customize the size of the shawl. The size is completely customizable by repeating chart B as many times as desired (diamonds and leaves), and chart C will line up with chart B regardless of how many repeats are worked.

Instead of binding off after finishing the charts, this shawl has an edge knit across the top of the shawl. This edge mimics the yo-garter stitch edging on the sides of the shawl, so that all three sides of the shawl look the same. This also makes the top edge more stretchy than if the shawl had just been bound off across the top, and the top edge will not pucker when blocked.
Since the pattern is stockinette based, the shawl has a garter stitch edging, 2 stitches wide, outside the yarn-overs to prevent it from curling. This means that the first and last two stitches of each WS-row are always knit.

MATERIALS

1 skein Zen Yarn Garden Serenity Silk [80% merino, 10% silk, 10% cashmere; 500 yds per 100 g] shown in Margarita
1 set 40 inch US 7 [4.5 mm] circular needles

GAUGE

18 sts and 24 rows = 4 in [10 cm] in pattern, blocked

FINISHED (BLOCKED) SIZE (with 3 repeats of Chart B)

Width: 68 inches [174 cm]
Height: 34 inches [87 cm]

INSTRUCTIONS

CO 2 sts using any non-provisional cast-on
Set up Row 1 (WS): K2
Set up Row 2 (RS): Kfb, kfb - 4 sts
Set up Row 3: K4
Start working chart A.
Repeat rows 63-94 on chart B as many times as desired for the size shawl you want, ending with a row 86. Then continue with chart C.
Chart C + the edging will add approx. 5 inches [12 cm] to the height of the shawl.

BORDER

After row 112 on Chart C, with RS facing, cast on an additional 5 sts using a cable cast-on. These sts will be used for a knit on border across the top, that will mimic the yo-garter stitch edges along the sides of the shawl. The border will be worked across 5 stitches, and every RS-row of the border will use up one stitch from the main body of the shawl.

28

Row 1(RS): K4, k2tog; turn
Row 2(WS): Sl1, k4; turn
Row 3: As 1
Row 4: As 2
Row 5: K2, yo, k2tog, k2tog; turn
Row 6: Sl1, p2, k2; turn

Repeat border rows 5-6 until only 2 unworked stitches remain from the main body of the shawl.
Then work border rows 1-3.
BO remaining 5 sts.
Sew in ends and block.

DELTA ANALYSIS

To analyze the chart in Margarita Leaves, start with the number of stitches at the end of the set-up section — 4 sts.

To calculate the delta for row 1, first convert the chart to written instructions:. Row 1 (as read from right to left):

    k2, yo, k2

Then substitute each stitch with the correct delta , like this:

k2	yo	k2
2*0	1	2*0

CHART A

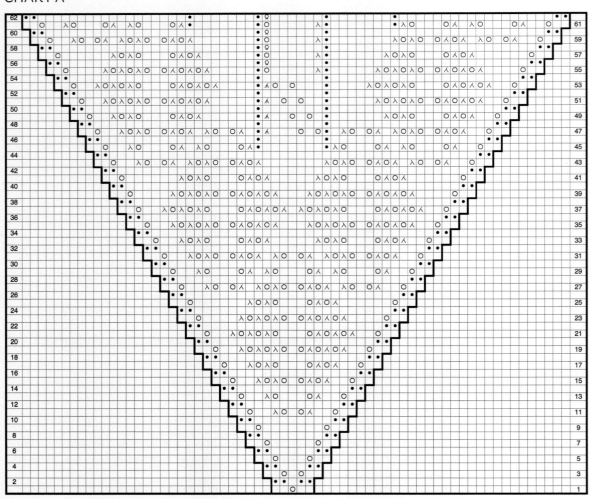

And finally add up the deltas for each stitch to get the total delta for the row. In this case, the sum is 1, which means that there is 1 more stitch on the needles than at the beginning of the row. So the total stitch count is now 5.

Row 2 has a total delta of 0, which means that there is no change in the total stitch count.
Row 3 (as read from right to left):

    k2, yo, k, yo, k2

Then substitute each stitch with the correct delta , like this:

k2	yo	k	yo	k2
2*0	1	0	1	2*0

And finally add up the deltas for each stitch to get the total delta for the row. In this case, the sum is 2, which means that there are 2 more stitches on the needles than at the beginning of the row. So the total stitch count is now 7.

Every RS-row in the pattern, starting at row 3, has a total delta of 2. And every WS-row in the pattern has a total delta of 0. This means that the stitch count increases by 2 on every RS-row, and stays constant on the WS-rows. This creates a triangle with two equal sides, starting with a 90 degree corner on the bottom point.

30

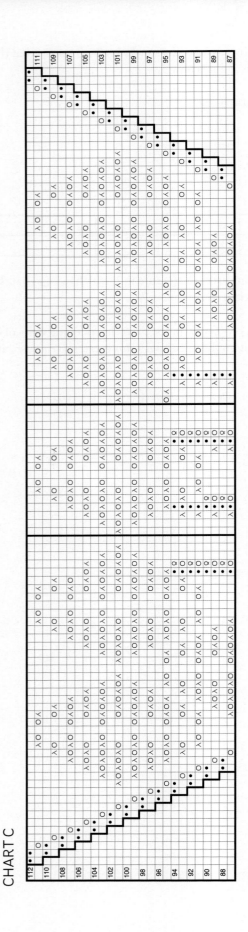

CHART C

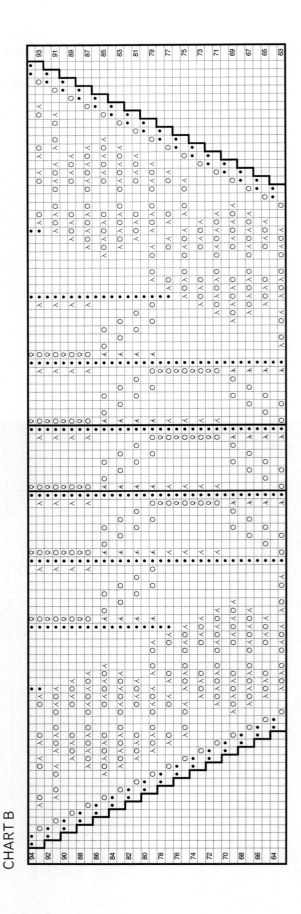

CHART B

Chapter FOUR:
Triangular shawls, neck-to-edge

Once we know how to knit one triangle, we can knit two side by side. This construction is probably the most common construction for triangular shawls. It starts by casting on a few stitches at the neck of the shawl, and the knitter works two triangles downwards and out. Similar to the bottom-up triangular shawl, you don't have to determine the size of the shawl prior to casting on, but can simply keep on knitting until you reach the desired size of shawl.

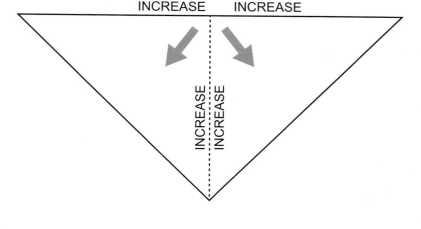

The neck-to-edge shawl tends to drape better than a bottom-up triangular shawl because of how the rows are oriented. A bottom-up triangular shawl stretches vertically when worn, which makes the bottom point of the triangle sharper than 90 degrees. A neck-to-edge triangular shawl stretches evenly in a V, so the overall shape of the triangle stays the same.

Any bottom-up triangular shawl can be converted to a neck-to-edge shawl by knitting the triangular chart twice. However, the final result will look quite different, and it will also be twice as large. The orientation of the lace motifs on a neck-to-edge shawl is upside down when worn as compared to when knit as a bottom-up triangle. So if it's a pictorial motif, make sure to knit it upside down. This also means that if you take the chart for the Margarita Leaves shawl in chapter three and use it for this type of shawl, your leaves would be upside down, and you would have a row of diamonds across the entire top edge of the shawl, as well as a center spine with diamonds on each side.

A very common way to set up this type of shawl is to have a 2 st garter-stitch border along the top, and one knit stitch separating the two triangles along the spine. The sample chart shows only one triangle, but the triangle is knit twice for the neck to edge construction. Right side rows are: K2, yo, charted-row, yo, k, yo, charted row, yo, k2. Wrong side rows are: K2, purl to the last 2 sts, k2.

In the sample chart (page 109), the center stitch is highlighted in order to aid in centering the motif.

Magic Lanterns

Magic Lanterns is inspired by the magical lamps and lanterns found all over the Grand Bazaar in Istanbul. The shawl is covered with a number of different lanterns, some glowing brighter and others with smaller pinprick lights. The lanterns spread from the top of the shawl towards the bottom. The warm glow of the lanterns then spread in a soft, wavy pattern and recede in the darkness. It starts at the nape of the neck with a few cast-on stitches, and is worked as two triangles outwards towards the lower edge. The main motif consists of a number of lanterns. The light glows differently inside the different lanterns — the first few have a larger light and a wick, and then next set have smaller pin-prick lights. The lanterns grow into one another, so this portion of the shawl (Charts A and B) could easily be repeated for a larger size shawl. The shawl is then finished with a wavy border, which is pulled into peaks when blocked. The last 3 rows are worked in garter stitch to stabilize the edge and prevent it from curling. It is worked from neck-to-edge.

MATERIALS

1 skein Spirit Trail Fiberworks Nona [50% merino, 25% bombyx silk, 25% cashmere; 640 yds per 115 g] shown in lilac
1 set 32 in US 6 [4 mm] circular needles
Optional: longer circular needles in the same size

GAUGE

14 sts and 26 rows = 4 in [10 cm] in pattern, blocked

FINISHED (BLOCKED) SIZE

Width: 72 in [182 cm]
Height: 36 in [91 cm]

INSTRUCTIONS

CO 5 sts using a cabled cast-on
Set up Row 1 (RS): K5
Set up Row 2 (WS): K5
Set up Row 3: K2, yo, k1, yo, k2 - 7 sts
Set up Row 4: K2, p3, k2
Each row in the pattern is worked:
K2, charted-row, k1, charted-row, k2
Begin chart A. Work rows 1 - 51 once, then rows 35 - 51 once, then rows 35-51 as many times as desired, each time adding a repeat of the sts in the box, and repeating the sts in the box twice on rows 71 - 77.
Work Chart B.
Chart C: Work rows 121 to 167

EDGING

After row 167 on Chart C, knit 3 rows. Then bind off as follows: K2, *return sts to left needle, k2tog through back loop, k1, repeat from * until no unworked stitches remain.
Sew in ends and block. When blocking, pull the ⑩ sts in row 165 to a peak.

CHART LEGEND NOTES

⑩ – work 3 sts as follows: insert rn into 3rd stitch on ln and pass over previous 2 sts, then k, yo, k

DELTA ANALYSIS

The special stitch ⑩ uses three stitches to make three stitches, so the delta is 0.
Each RS row in the charts has a total delta of +2, which means that the chart grows by 2 stitches on every right side row.
Each RS row in the pattern is worked as follows:
K2, charted-row, k, charted-row, k2

Unlike the sample chart, in this chapter, the increases are incorporated in the chart. Note that the first and last stitch of each charted row is a yo without a matching decrease. The exceptions are rows 29, 47, 83 and 101 where the unmatched yo's are the second stitch and the second to last one. The reason for shifting the unmatched yo in one stitch is to keep the lantern pattern going. Since it's still so close to the edge, it doesn't affect the overall shaping of the shawl.

Aside from the unmatched yarn overs on the right side rows, each increase in the lace patterning must have a matching decrease. The total stitch count grows by 4 on every right-side row — one stitch near the beginning of the row, one stitch on each side of the spine, and one stitch near the end of the row.

CHART A

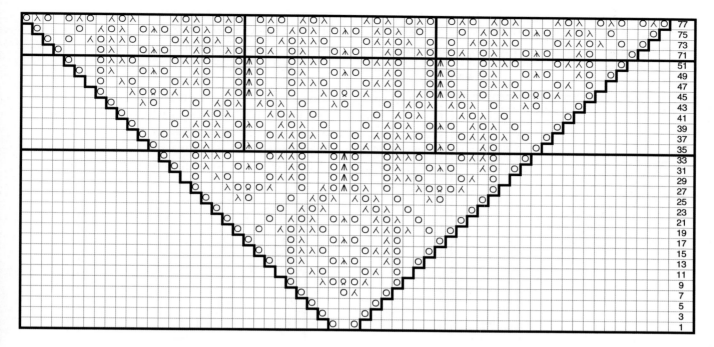

To calculate the delta for row 1, consider the fact that row 1 is worked as follows:

    K2, charted-row1, k1, charted-row1, k2

This means that the delta for row 1 is equal to the sum or the deltas of the instructions.

    Delta(row 1) = delta(k2) + delta(charted-row 1) + delta(k1) + delta(charted-row 1) +
    delta(k2)

First we calculate the delta for charted-row 1. Convert charted-row 1 to written instructions as follows:

    Yo, k1, yo

Substitute each stitch with the correct delta:

yo	k	yo
1	0	1

And add up the deltas for each stitch to get the delta for the charted-row.

    Delta(charted-row 1) = 2

Then it's time to calculate the total delta of the row as follows:

k2	CR1	k	CR1	k2
2*0	2	0	2	2*0

And finally add up the deltas for each stitch to get the total delta for the row. In this case, the sum is 4, which means that there are 4 more stitches on the needles than at the beginning of the row. So the total stitch count is now 11.

This type of shawl could also be constructed by casting on lots and lots of stitches along the V edge and decreasing four stitches on every right-side row — one at the beginning of the row, one on either side of the center stitch and one at the end of the row. Again, this construction requires the designer to predetermine the size of the finished shawl, and making sure that there is enough yarn available to fill the entire triangle. Also, there is no way of changing your mind and making the shawl larger at the end, if you find yourself with extra yarn.

It is also possible to make a more complicated design by charting two different triangles — one for the left side of the shawl and one for the right side of the shawl. In more practical terms, this isn't done very often, as symmetry is visually pleasing, but of course it would be possible to have a neck-to-edge triangular shawl with a leaf pattern on one side and a diamond pattern on the other side.

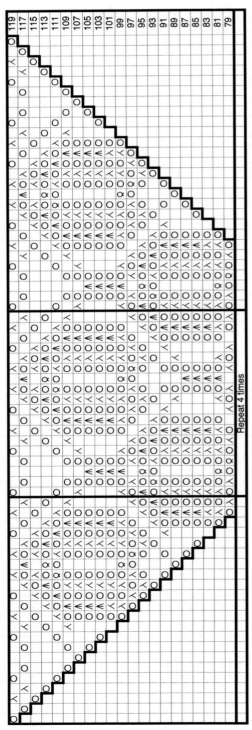

CHART C

CHART B

Repeat 6 times

Repeat 4 times

Chapter FIVE:
Creating additional canvas space on triangular shawls for visual interest

The bottom-up and neck-to-edge triangular shawl constructions are very common, and account for most of the triangular shawl patterns available. But if you would like to create something that is a little bit different, you can play with the construction a bit to create additional canvas space on your triangular shawl. In the basic bottom-up triangular shawl we worked the yarn-overs near the edges of the shawl — with only a couple of garter-stitches as an edging. But if you shift the increases in by several stitches, you can create additional canvas space border-

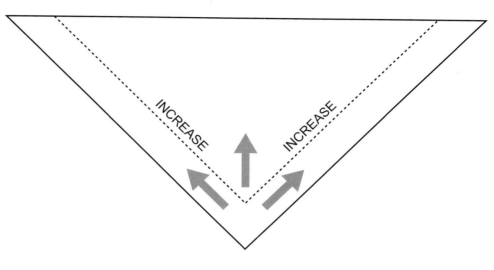

ing the main canvas. By using a different lace pattern on this border you can make a shawl that looks more interesting than just a regular bottom-up shawl. The lace pattern on the border will be at a 45 degree angle as compared to the main shawl.

For a neck-to-edge triangular shawl you can create additional canvas space both along the top and down the center spine of the shawl. Again, this is accomplished by shifting the point of increase on the row. So on each right-side row, start with lace edge, increase stitch count with one, work triangular canvas, increase stitch count with one, work center lace pattern, increase stitch count with one, work triangular canvas, increase stitch count with one, work lace edge.

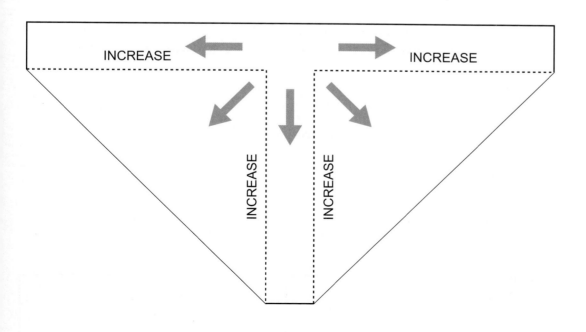

Mystic Roses

In Mystic Roses , a neck-to-edge triangular lace shawl with a large lace pattern in the center and along the top edge, the lace pattern along the top edge and in the center is 23 stitches wide. The lace pattern itself depicts the stem of a rose with leaves on both sides. It is distinctly different from the lace pattern on the main canvas of the shawl, and adds visual interest to the shawl. The main canvas is covered with little rosebuds, created with a combination of lace and mini-cables. As you work towards the lower edges though, the pattern along the top edge and in the center is picked up in the main canvas to create the impression of a border that matches the spine and the top.

MATERIALS

1 skein Wollmeise Lace-Garn [100% wool; 1740 yds per 300 g skein] shown in Rosenrot
1 set 47 in US 5 [3.75 mm] needles
Cable needle

GAUGE

16 sts and 28 rows = 4 in [10 cm] in pattern, blocked

FINISHED SIZES

The finished height is approximately 134 cm (52"), and the wingspan is 268 cm (105").
There is also a small version of the shawl available.

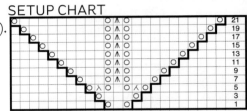

SETUP CHART

SETUP

CO 9 sts using a cabled cast-on
Set up Row 1(RS): K9 Set up Row 2(WS): K2, p5, k2
The next 22 rows are knit as follows:
Right side: K2, work setup-chart, k1, setup-chart, k1, setup-chart, k2
Wrong side: K2, purl until 2 stitches remain, k2
After the setup instructions, you will have 3 triangles on your needles — like this.

The rest of the shawl will be worked as follows:
Right side rows: k2, left side, ChartXleft, center, ChartXright, right-side, k2
Wrong side rows: k2, purl to the last 2 stitches, k2
The left side, center and right-side charts consist of 20 rows that will be repeated as the shawl grows.

You will note that the three charts are very similar. The difference lies in the decreases in the two first and two last columns of your chart.

For reference, each section of the shawl will be broken up into a right chart, a left chart and a lace panel with the main part of the side- and center-patterns. I found it very useful when lining up the side- and center-patterns to the main chart. However, the lace

RIGHT   CENTER   LEFT

panel reference chart will include all the decreases. You must SHAWL OVERVIEW
remember that they are actually knit differently depending
on whether it is used for the left side, center or right-side.

LARGE VERSION OF MYSTIC ROSES

Work the body of the shawl using charts A-D. Then work
chart E. Note that for Chart E, the left, center and right-
side charts are included, and should be worked as written.
Row 234: K2, purl to the last 2 sts, k2
Proceed to the finishing instructions.

SMALL VERSION OF MYSTIC ROSES

Work the body of the shawl using charts A-C, but stop at
row 112. After row 112, work chart F-G.
Note that for Chart G, the left, center and right-side charts are included, and should be worked as written.
Row 194: K2, purl to the last 2 sts, k2
Proceed to the finishing instructions.

FINISHING INSTRUCTIONS

Turn the work and bind off as follows: K2, *return sts to left needle, k2tog through back loop, k1, repeat from * until no unworked
stitches remain.
Sew in ends and block. When blocking, pull each of the shaded YOs on the last row of the chart to a point for the edging.

DELTA ANALYSIS

The actual increases for each right-side row is built into the lace pattern in the edging/center patterns. The center chart has an unmatched yarn-over at the beginning and the end of each right-side row.

So when analyzing the delta of the first row of the center chart, first convert the chart to written instructions:
Row 1 (as read from right to left):

    yo, k4, k2tog, k3, yo, k3, yo, k3, ssk, k4, yo

Then substitute each stitch with the correct delta , like this:

yo	k4	k2tog	k3	yo	k3	yo	k3	ssk	k4	yo
1	4*0	-1	3*0	1	3*0	1	3*0	-1	4*0	1

And finally add up the deltas for each stitch to get the total delta for the row. In this case, the sum is 2, which means that the stitch
count grows by two stitches on every row. But the extra stitch isn't used in the center chart on the next row, but rather by the main
chart (which grows like a triangle)

The left side chart and right side chart have an unmatched yarn-over each on the inside edge (touching the main canvas) for the
same reason. The outer edge is worked with a matching decrease in order to get a straight edge along the top of the shawl.
The set-up for the Mystic Roses shawl is a little bit different as well. Basically you work three triangles for 21 rows, similar to how a
neck-to-edge shawl is constructed, but with three triangles instead of two, and then these three triangles form the base for the left-
and right-side edgings, as well as the center spine. As illustrated in the schematic, this means that the shawl has a slight dip right at
the neck, which makes it fit nicely when worn.

44

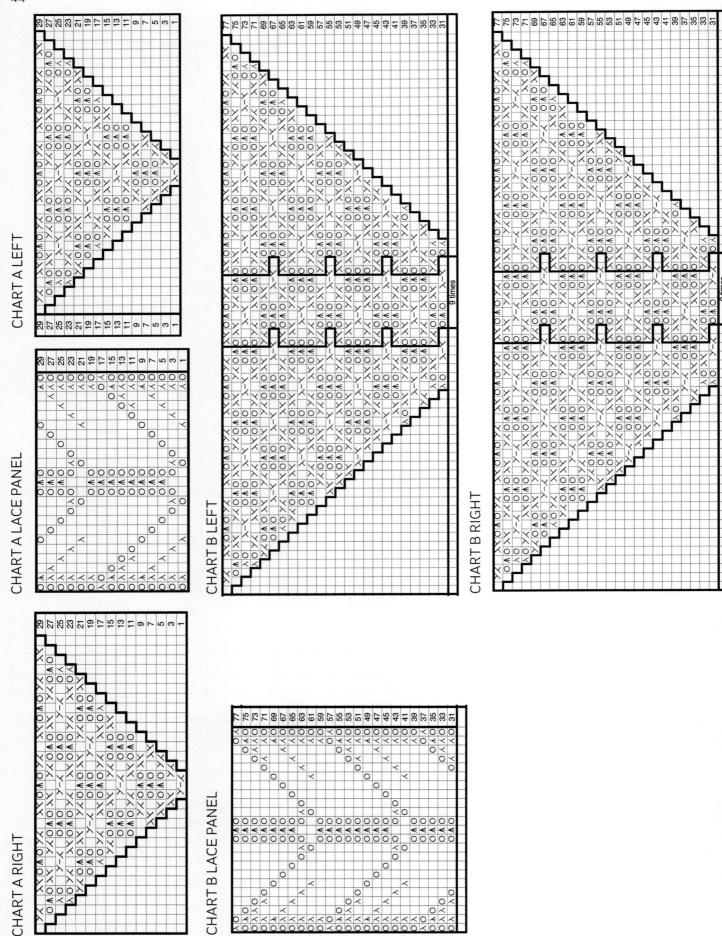

CHART A LEFT

CHART A LACE PANEL

CHART A RIGHT

CHART B LEFT

9 times

CHART B RIGHT

9 times

CHART B LACE PANEL

CHART C LEFT

CHART C LACE PANEL

CHART C RIGHT

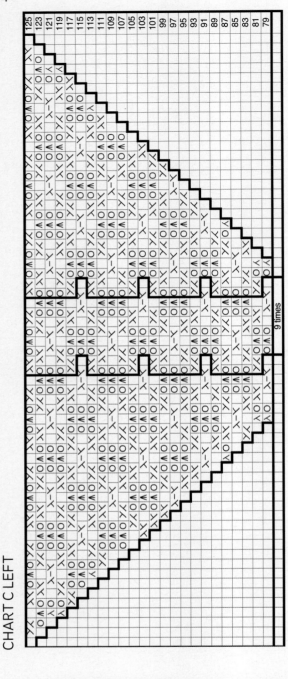

CHART D LEFT

CHART D RIGHT

CHART D LACE PANEL

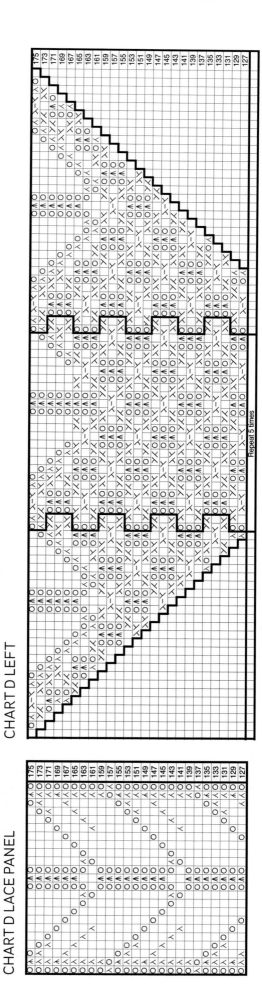

48

CHART E

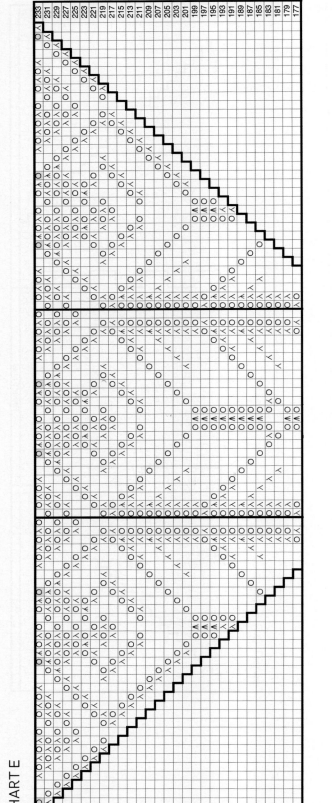

CHART E LACE RIGHT

CHART E LACE CENTER

CHART E LACE LEFT

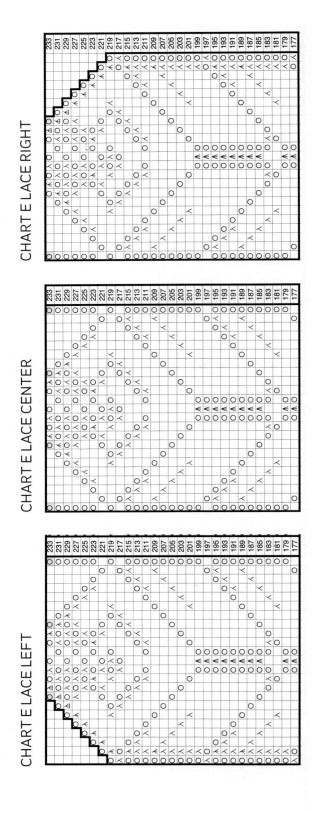

49

SMALL CHART F LEFT

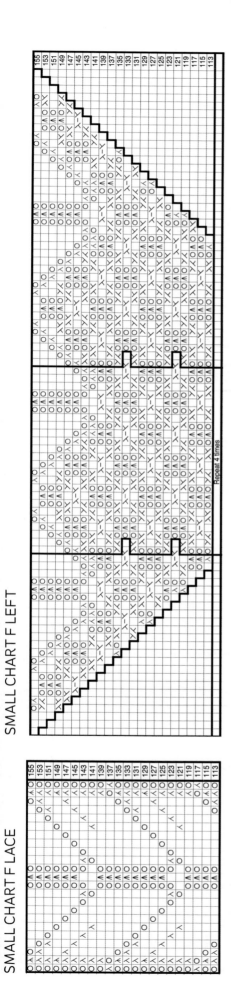

SMALL CHART F LACE

SMALL CHART F RIGHT

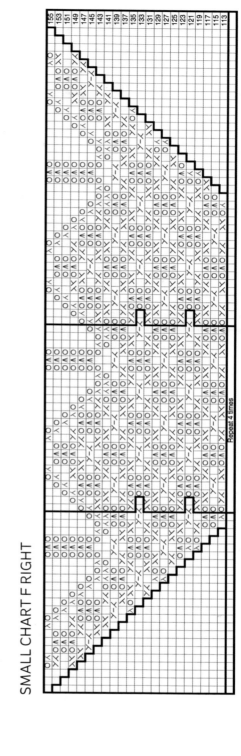

SMALL CHART G

Repeat 6 times

SMALL CHART G LACE RIGHT

SMALL CHART G LACE

SMALL CHART G LACE LEFT

Chapter SIX:

Variations on triangular shawls

- Shallow triangles knit from bottom-up
- Shallow triangles knit from side to side
- Shallow triangles knit from neck-to-edge

With the basic triangular shawls that were covered in chapters three and four, we can create a number of other types of triangular shawls if we just play with the rate of increase a little bit. To recap, in chapter 3 we learned how to make a basic, bottom-up triangle by increasing the stitch count by 2 on every right side row (one stitch at the beginning of the row and one stitch at the end of the row). It is of course possible to increase at a different rate, in order to get a different slope to the triangle.

SWATCH 3

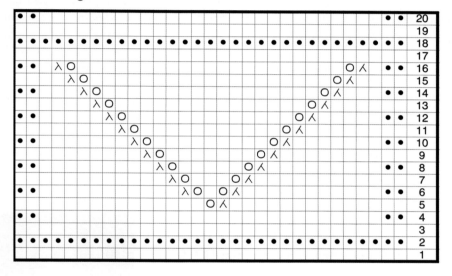

For example, this swatch shows a V of yarn-overs leaning towards the outside at a 22.5 degree angle (half of 45 degrees). The V is created by shifting the yarn-overs one stitch to the outside on every row (RS and WS). This looks like the bottom edges of a triangular shawl. Therefore, in order to create a triangular shawl from the bottom-up, start with a small number of stitches and grow each row with one stitch at the beginning of each right-side row, and one stitch at the end of each right-side row.

Alternatively it is possible to achieve the same shape of the shawl by increasing each row with two stitches at the beginning of each right-side row, and two stitches at the end of each right-side row.

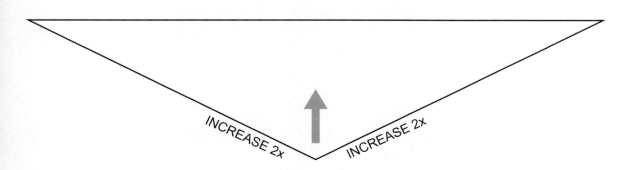

Tidal Waves

BOTTOM UP SHAPING

In Tidal Waves the shawl grows by a total of 4 stitches on every right-side row — 2 stitches at the beginning of the row and two stitches at the end of the row. Every right-side row starts with k2, yo, yo and ends with yo, yo, k2. Every wrong-side row is k3, purl to the last three stitches, k3. This means that the double yarn-overs will have two stitches worked into it. Each double yarn-over is shown as two stitches on the chart, and on the next row first knit into the yarn-over, and then purl into the second loop of the yarn-over at the beginning of the WS-row. Then purl all stitches until you have 3 stitches left on the ln. The last stitch you worked (with a purl) was the first loop of the double yarn-over. Then knit into the second loop of the double yarn-over and knit the last two stitches.

The lace motif itself is fairly simple. Notice that starting on row 5 the yarn-overs are separated from their matching decreases by two stitches. What this accomplishes is to slant the stitches between the yo and the matching decrease. So on the finished piece you will notice straight columns of stockinette stitches growing from the bottom of the triangle, and then the two stitches between the yo/decrease combinations will be leaning at a 45 degree angle to the straight column. These two stitches between the lace patterning form the tidal waves, running from the top edge towards the bottom of the shawl. The eye is drawn to the solid part of the shawl (the "negative space") and can pick out the waves between the lace patterning (the holes).

The size of the Tidal Waves shawl can be adjusted, by simply repeating rows 17-27 as many times as desired. To finish the shawl off, work the last few rows to complete the lace pattern and then bind off.

The Tidal Waves run from the top of the shawl to the bottom of the shawl, twisting and turning between the rocks and obstacles that are depicted in the lace pattern.

MATERIALS

1 skein Handmaiden Swiss Mountain Sea Sock
[51% silk, 29% Merino, 20% plant fiber; 437 yds
per 100g skein] Shown in Topaz
1 set 40 in US 6 [4 mm] circular needles
Large-eyed, blunt needle
Clip on stitch marker

GAUGE

16 sts and 28 rows = 4 in [10cm] in pattern,
blocked
Finished (Blocked) Size:
Width: 68 in [193 cm]
Height: 18 in [46 cm] with 7 repeats
Both height and width are dependent on the number of repeats.

INSTRUCTIONS

CO 5 sts using a cabled cast-on
Set up Row 1 (RS): K5
Set up Row 2 (WS): K5
Set up Row 3: K2, yo, yo, k1, yo, yo, k2 - 9 sts
Set up Row 4: K3, p3, k3
Start working the chart.

Note that only RS-rows are charted.

All WS-rows are k3, purl to the last 3 stitches, k3.

Work rows 1-16

Work rows 15-28, and repeat as many times as desired for the size of shawl you would like.

For each time you repeat rows 15-28, work the stitches in the central box 2 additional times.

After final repeat, work rows 29-40

FINISHING INSTRUCTIONS

Row 41: K2, yo, yo, k to the last 2 sts, yo, yo, k2

Row 42: K3, purl to the last 3 sts, k3

Rows 43-44: As rows 41-42

Locate the center stitch and mark it with a clip-on stitch marker.

Row 44: K2, yo, yo, [k2tog, yo] repeat until center stitch, k1, [yo, ssk] repeat until 2 sts remain, yo, yo, k2

Row 45: K3, p, k to the last 4 sts, p, k3

Rows 46-47: Knit

Bind off as follows: K2, *return sts to ln, k2tog through back loop, k1, repeat from * until no unworked stitches remain. Break yarn, pass through last st, and tighten.

Sew in ends and block.

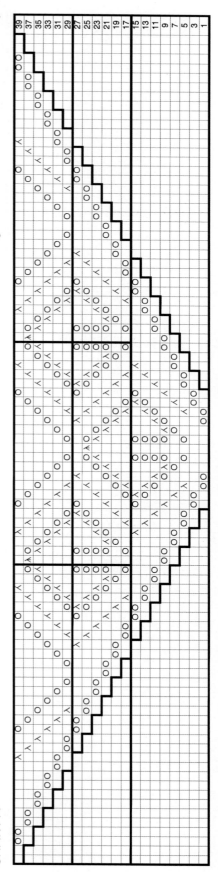

CHART A

Changing Directions

SWATCH 4

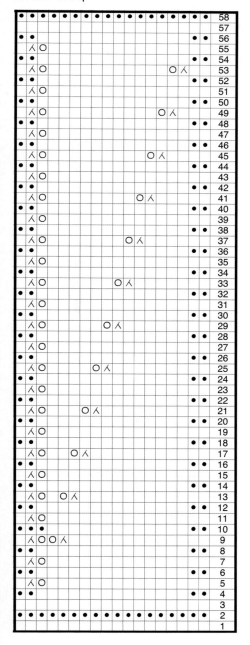

SIDE TO SIDE SHAPING

In chapter 3 and 4 we knit triangles starting at the bottom and starting at the top. But it is also possible to make a triangle by starting at a side corner and work towards the other side corner. In that case, one side of the knitting has no shaping at all — this will form the long edge across the top of the shawl — and all the shaping takes place on the side of the knitting that will form the bottom point.

In order to knit a sideways triangular shawl with a 90 degree point at the bottom, cast on a few stitches and increase the stitch count by one at the beginning of every right-side row. This means that the angle between the top of the shawl and the bottom edge is 45 degrees. Continue working in this fashion until you have reached the deepest point of the shawl (or used up half of your yarn). Then for the second half of the shawl, the stitch count decreases by one at the beginning of every right-side row.

This swatch shows a wedge created between a vertical line of yarn-overs, and a diagonal line of yarn-overs leaning towards the right side at a 22.5 degree angle compared to the vertical line. This wedge looks like the side-point of a shallow triangular shawl.

The Changing Directions shawl is a great shawl for people at a cross roads. Time to do something new? Knit yourself this shawl as a talisman and secret support to help you reach your goals and dreams.

MATERIALS

1 skein Rocky Mountain Dyeworks Glacier Ice [70% alpaca, 30% silk; 870 yds per 100g] shown in Calendula
1 set 32 inch US 1.5 [2.5 mm] circular needles
Stitch marker
Large-eyed, blunt needle

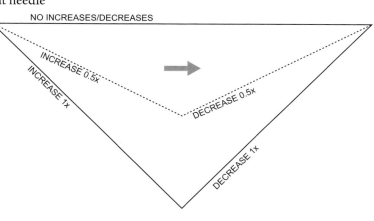

NO INCREASES/DECREASES
INCREASE 0.5x
INCREASE 1x
DECREASE 0.5x
DECREASE 1x

GAUGE

24 sts and 34 rows = 4 in [10cm] in garter stitch, blocked

FINISHED (BLOCKED) SIZE

Width: 94 in [240 cm]
Height: 21 in [54 cm]

INSTRUCTIONS

CO 8 sts using a cabled cast-on
Set up Rows 1-4: K8
Start working chart A, noting that row 1 is a RS row.

Note that all rows are charted. All RS rows are worked from right to left. All WS rows are worked from left to right.

Work charts A and B. Then work chart C as many times as desired, each time adding a repeat of the stitches in the box. Work chart D once, repeating the stitches in the box as many times as in the last iteration of chart C. Work chart E as many times as you worked chart C, each time removing a repeat of the stitches in the box. Work charts F and G.
For the sample, chart C was worked six times.

FINISHING INSTRUCTIONS

Knit four rows, then bind off as follows: K2, *return sts to ln, k2tog through back loop, k1, repeat from * until 1 st remains. Break off yarn, thread through last st and secure.
Sew in ends and block.

DELTA ANALYSIS

Changing Directions starts on one side point with only 8 stitches. The stitch count then increases by 1 every 4 rows on the right edge of the knitting. The (angled) right edge will form the bottom edge of the finished shawl, and the (straight) left edge will form the top edge of the finished shawl. Changing Directions is a garter-based lace pattern, with lace patterning on every row. The first four stitches of every row are: k2, yo, k2tog and the last four stitches of every row are yo, k2tog, k2. This forms a nice edging with a column of staggered yarn-overs called faggoting. The shaping of the shawl occurs on the 5th stitch of every other right-side row (rows 5, 9, 13, etc). For the first half of the shawl, there is an extra increase (yarn-over).

To calculate the delta for row 5, first convert the chart to written instructions:
Row 5 (as read from right to left):

    K2, yo, k2tog, yo, k, yo, k2tog, k

Then substitute each stitch with the correct delta , like this:

k2	yo	k2tog	yo	k	yo	k2tog	k
2*0	1	-1	1	0	1	-1	0

And finally add up the deltas for each stitch to get the total delta for the row. In this case, the sum is 1, which means that there is 1 more stitch on the needles than at the beginning of the row.

To calculate the delta on row 6, first convert the chart to written instructions.
Row 6 (worked from left to right on the chart):

    K2, yo, k2tog, ktbl, k, yo, k2tog, k

ktbl has a delta of 0 as it uses one stitch from the ln and creates one stitch on the rn.
Substitute each stitch with the correct delta:

k2	yo	k2tog	ktbl	k	yo	k2tog	k
2*0	1	-1	0	0	1	-1	0

And add up the deltas for each stitch to get the total delta for the row. The sum is 0, which means the stitch count stayed constant on this row.

If you continue to calculate the delta for each row, you will find that rows 5, 9, 13, etc up to row 173 each have a delta of 1, and all other rows have a delta of 0.

When you reach half the length of the desired shawl, the stitch count starts to decrease on every 4th row. Starting on row 181 (and rows 185, 189, 193, etc), the 5th stitch is an unmatched k2tog.

To calculate the delta on row 181, first convert the chart to written instructions:

Row 181:

K2, yo, k2tog, k2tog, k4, k2tog, yo, k, yo, ssk, k, k2tog, yo, k, yo, ssk, k, k2tog, yo, k, yo, ssk, k, k2tog, yo, k, yo, ssk, k, k2tog, yo, k, yo, ssk, k, k2tog, yo, k, yo, ssk, k3, yo, k2tog, k

Substitute each stitch with the correct delta:

k2	yo	k2tog	k2tog	k4	k2tog	yo	k	yo	ssk	k	k2tog	yo
2*0	1	-1	-1	4*0	-1	1	0	1	-1	0	-1	1
k	yo	ssk	k	k2tog	yo	k	yo	ssk	k	k2tog	yo	k
0	1	-1	-1	-1	0	1	-1	0	-1	1	0	1
yo	ssk	k	k2tog	yo	k	yo	ssk	k	k2tog	yo	k	yo
1	-1	0	-1	1	0	1	-1	0	-1	1	0	1
ssk	k3	yo	k2tog	k								
-1	3*0	1	-1	0								

And add up the deltas for each stitch to get the total delta for the row. The sum is -1, which means the stitch count decreased by one on this row, just as expected.

If you continue to calculate the delta for each row after the center, you will find that rows 181, 185, 189, 193 etc up to row 353 each have a delta of -1, and all other rows have a delta of 0.

CHART A

CHART B

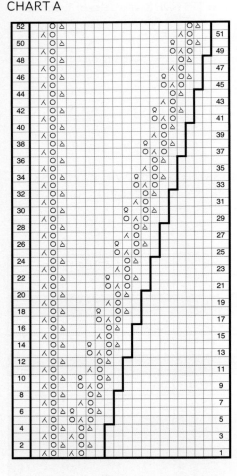

CHANGING DIRECTIONS LEGEND

The legend for Changing Directions is different as it is worked in garter stitch:

□ – k on rs and ws
⋏ – k2tog on rs
λ – ssk on rs
⊿ – k2tog on ws
◿ – ssk on ws
⋀ – k3tog on rs
⩕ – k3tog on ws
⋀ – sl2 sts together, knitwise, k, pssso
O – yo
Ọ – ktbl

CHART C

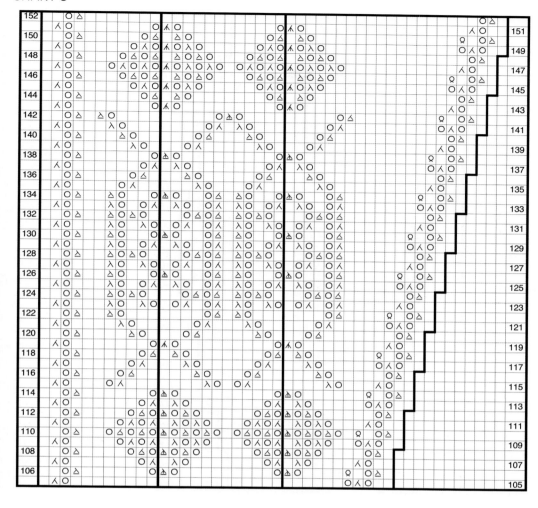

62

CHART D

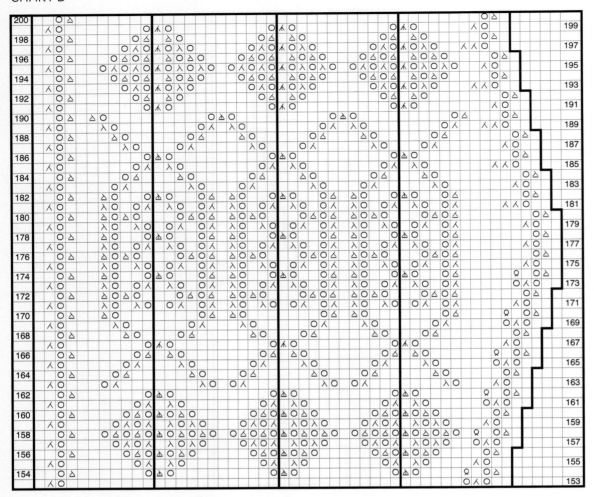

CHART E

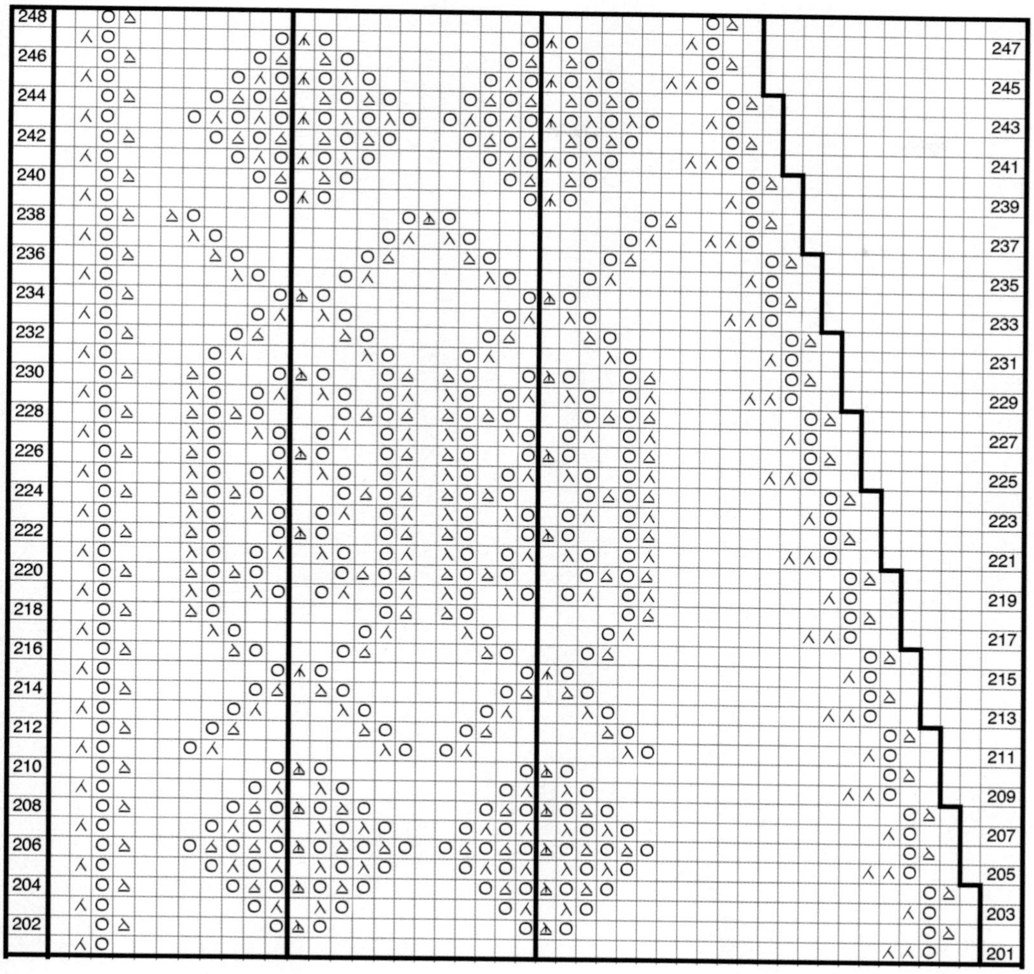
248
246
244
242
240
238
236
234
232
230
228
226
224
222
220
218
216
214
212
210
208
206
204
202
247
245
243
241
239
237
235
233
231
229
227
225
223
221
219
217
215
213
211
209
207
205
203
201

CHART F

CHART G

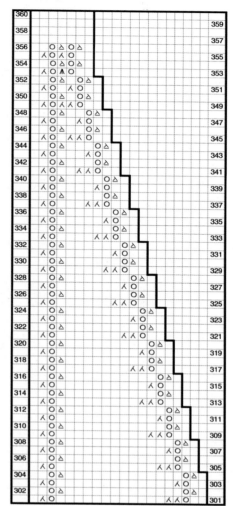

Chandelier Shawl

NECK-TO-EDGE SHAPING

Another possibility is to modify a neck-to-edge triangle and play with the rate of increase there. As you recall from Chapter 4, a neck-to-edge triangle consists of two triangles next to each other, separated by a center column of knit stitches, often referred to as the spine of the shawl. The Chandelier Shawl is a crescent shaped shawl knit from the neck to the bottom edge. As in chapter 4, the shawl starts at the neck and increases at the beginning, center and the end of each right-side row. However, unlike the regular tri-angular shawl in chapter 4, this crescent type shawl increases with 2 stitches at the beginning of each right-side row, one on either side of the center stitch, and 2 stitches at the end of the row, for a total of 6 new stitches every row.

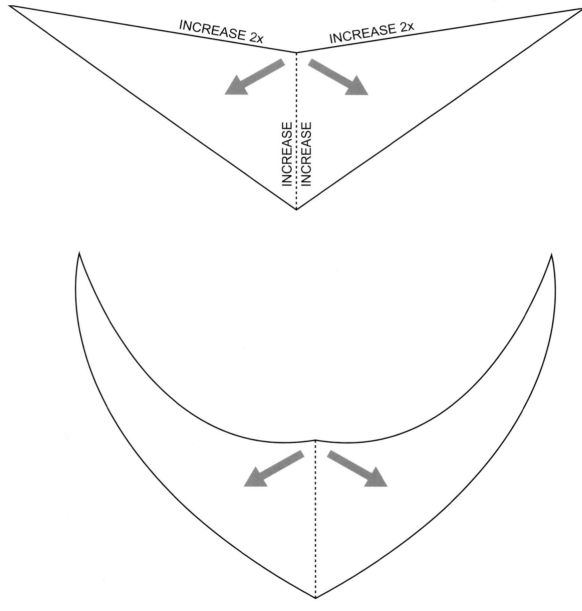

The shawl can be blocked either to a crescent shape, with a curve across the top, or the top can be blocked straight. The curve looks more appealing though, and the edge has a tendency to curve naturally with the two yarn-overs so close to the edge. A stretchy bind-off is essential, since the bound off edge will be stretched a little bit extra to accommodate the curve. For the Chandelier

Shawl, the stretchy outer edge has been emphasized by the last pattern row where the yarn overs do not have any matching decreases. This means that the stitch count increases drastically on the last pattern row, which allows us to block the shawl into a crescent with the rounded outer edge. It also allows us to pull the outer edge to peaks while blocking, without putting too much strain on the outer edge, since there are several extra stitches available.

The Chandelier Shawl's crescent shape and patterning is meant to evoke light radiating out from the top of the shawl towards the edges. The light is layered as if cascading from a chandelier.

MATERIALS

1 skein Slackford Studio Nimbus Cloud [70% baby alpaca, 10% cashmere, 20% silk; 400 yds per 100 g] shown in True Blood
1 set 40 in US 6 [4 mm] circular needles
Large-eyed, blunt needle
Stitch marker

GAUGE

16 sts and 24 rows = 4 in [10cm] in stockinette, blocked

FINISHED (BLOCKED) SIZE

Wingspan: 63 in [160 cm]
Height: 26 in [67 cm]

INSTRUCTIONS

CO 5 sts using a cabled cast-on
Set up Row 1(RS): K2, PM, k3
Set up Row 2(WS): K5

Row 1: K2, yo, slip marker, k1, yo, k2
Row 2: K2, p3 sts, k2
Row 3: K2, yo, yo, knit to marker, yo, slip marker, k1, yo, k to last 2 sts, yo, yo, k2
Row 4: K3, purl to last 3 sts, k3
Rows 5-46: Repeat rows 3 & 4
At the end of row 46, you should have 139 sts on the needles.
Start working the charts.

Note that only RS-rows are charted.
All RS-rows are: k2, chart x.1, k, chart x.2, k2
All WS-rows are k3, purl to the last 3 stitches, k3.

FINISHING INSTRUCTIONS

Row 105 (RS): K2, yo, yo, k7, [yo, k1, yo, k7] 18 times, yo, k3, yo, k1, yo, k3, yo, [k7, yo, k1, yo] 18 times, k7, yo, yo, k2 - 393 sts
Row 106 (WS): K3, p1, k to the last 4 sts, p1, k3
Row 107-108: Knit all sts

Bind off as follows: K2, *return sts to left needle, k2tog through back loop, k1, repeat from * until no unworked stitches remain. Sew in ends and block.

DELTA ANALYSIS

To calculate the delta for row 103, consider the fact that row 103 is worked as follows:

Row 103: K2, charted-row B.1, k, charted-row B.2, k2

This means that the delta for row 103 is equal to the sum or the deltas of the instructions.

$$\text{Delta(row 103)} = \text{delta(K2)} + \text{delta(charted-row B.1)} + \text{delta(k)} + \text{delta(charted-row B.2)} + \text{delta(k2)}$$

First we calculate the delta for charted-row 103 on chart B.1. Convert row 103 on chart B.1 to written instructions as follows:
Row 103.B1: Yo, yo, k4, yo, sl2-k-psso, yo, k5, yo, sl2-k-psso, yo, k5, yo, sl2-k-psso, yo, k5, yo, sl2-k-psso, yo, k5, yo, sl2-k-psso, yo, k5, yo, ssk, k, yo

Substitute each stitch with the correct delta:

yo	yo	k4	yo	⋏	yo	k5	yo	⋏	yo	k5	yo	⋏
1	1	4*0	1	-2	1	5*0	1	-2	1	5*0	1	-2
yo	k5	yo	⋏	yo	k5	yo	⋏	yo	k5	yo	⋏	yo
1	5*0	1	-2	1	5*0	1	-2	1	5*0	1	-2	1
k5	yo	ssk	k	yo								
5*0	1	-1	0	1								

And add up the deltas for each stitch to get the total delta for the row. The sum is 3, which means that row 103 on chart B.1 has 3 stitches more than row 102 — which is exactly what we would expect, since the shaping of a crescent shawl means that we have to increase 2 stitches at the beginning of the row and 1 stitch just before the center stitch.

Then we calculate the delta for charted-row 103 on chart B.2

Row 103.B2: Yo, k, k2tog, yo, k5, yo, sl2-k-psso, yo, k5, yo, sl2-k-psso, yo, k5, yo, sl2-k-psso, yo, k5, yo, sl2-k-psso, yo, k5, yo, sl2-k-psso, k5, yo, sl2-k-psso, yo, k4, yo, yo

Substitute each stitch with the correct delta:

yo	k	k2tog	yo	k5	yo	⋏	yo	k5	yo	⋏	yo	k5
1	0	-1	1	5*0	1	-2	1	5*0	1	-2	1	5*0
yo	⋏	yo	k5	yo	⋏	yo	k5	yo	⋏	yo	k5	yo
1	-2	1	5*0	1	-2	1	5*0	1	-2	1	5*0	1
⋏	yo	k4	yo	yo								
-2	1	4*0	1	1								

Add up the deltas for each stitch to get the total delta of 3, which means that row 103 on chart B.2 also has 3 stitches more than row 102 — which again is what we were expecting.

So to calculate the total delta for row 103, remember that the row is written as follows:
Row 103: K2, charted-row B1.103, k, charted-row B2.103, k2
Substitute each part of the row with the correct delta:

k2	B1.103	k	B2.103	k2
2*0	3	0	3	2*0

Add up the deltas, for a total of 6. So far, so good — since for the crescent shaped shawl we must increase our stitch count by 6 on every right side row.

Row 105 deviates from this pattern.

Row 105 (rs): K2, yo, yo, k7, [yo, k, yo, k7] 18 times, yo, k3, yo, k, yo, k3, yo, [k7, yo, k, yo] 18 times, k7, yo, yo, k2

Substitute each part of the row with the correct delta:

k2	yo	yo	k7	yo	k	yo	k7	yo	k3	yo	k	yo
2*0	1	1	7*0	1	0	1	7*0	1	3*0	1	0	1
k3	yo	k7	yo	k	yo	k7	yo	yo	k2			
3*0	1	7*0	1	0	1	7*0	1	1	2*0			

Note that the stitches highlighted in red are repeated 18 times.

Add up the delta for each stitch, making sure to multiply each of the delta in the repeated section by 18, and the total is 80.

This means that row 105 has 80 stitches more than row 104. The shaping only accounts for 6 of these stitches. The rest will serve to make the edging more stretchy so it doesn't pucker at all when we block it and pull high peaks.

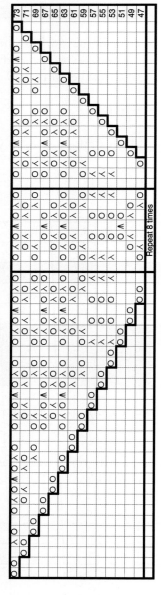

CHART A2

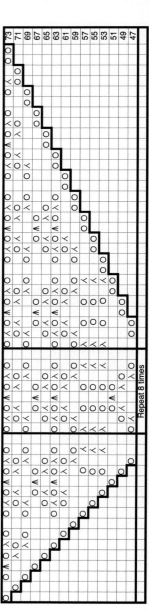

CHART A1

CHART B2

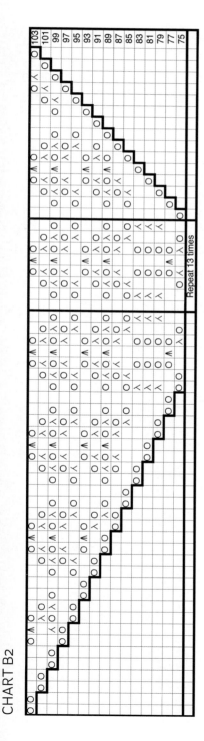

CHART B1

73

Chapter SEVEN:
edging on rectangular shawls (knit with shawl)

After our foray into triangular shawls, we now return to rectangular ones. As you recall from chapter 2, for a straight rectangular shawl we cast on the number of stitches required for the desired width or our rectangular shawl and never change the stitch count. However, we can add complexity or visual interest to our rectangular shawl by knitting an edging along with the shawl.

One way an edging can be created is by building triangles on each side of the rectangle that makes up the main canvas of a rectangular stole. First increase the stitch count by one stitch at the beginning and at the end of the row for X rows, and then decrease the stitch count by one stitch at the beginning and at the end of the row for X rows.

This is the same technique used as when knitting a triangle from side-to-side (chapter 6).

The stitch count should increase by one on every other row until the peak has been reached, and then decrease by one until we're back in the "valley".

While it would be possible to increase using a single yo, and then decrease using a k2tog or ssk, this would result in a diagonal line of holes along the increasing edge, and no holes along the decreasing edge. If this is the look you are going for, that's of course ok, but often we would like the line of holes to continue, so that both increasing and decreasing edges look similar. Consider using yo while increasing and some combination of a yo and decreases so that the line of holes continues, e.g. "k2tog, yo, k2tog" or "yo, k3tog". Either of these combinations result in a delta of -1.

In Blueberry Patch the bottom border is worked first. The bottom border starts with a provisional cast-on and then the right edge of the border stays straight, and the left edge grows as a triangle until row 11, and then shrinks at the same rate. There is a decorative line of three yarn-overs that follow the shaping of the edging.

Each right-side row between rows 3-11 contain three yarn-overs and only two decreases (k2togs). This means that the delta for the row is +1; that is to say, the stitch count grows by one on each of these rows. The right-side rows 13-19 and 1 contain three yarn-overs and four decreases (ssk-s). This means that the delta for each of those rows is -1; that is to say, the stitch count decreases by one on each of these rows.

After working 9 repeats of the bottom border chart, pick up stitches along the straight edge of the border, and from the provisional cast-on end. This provides the setup for the rest of the shawl. The stitches picked up along the straight edge of the border (in this case 91 stitches) provide the stitches for the rectangular canvas of the stole. The 11 stitches on either side will be worked as a border along with the body of the stole. The border will first increase its stitch count by one for five RS-rows, and then decrease its stitch count by one for the next five RS-rows.

The entire body of the shawl will be knit in this fashion. When the desired length of the shawl is reached, the "top" edge of the body will be capped with another border, similar to the bottom border. This closes off the shawl and works all the stitches across the top. The resulting stole has no cast-on edge and no bound-off edge.

Blueberry Patch

Finding a wild blueberry patch in the forest is one of the most amazing things. At first you are delighted to have found one blueberry, and you might think there is only one. Then you see one more. And one more. Until your eye adjusts and finds the delicious clusters hiding underneath the leaves. Blueberry Patch is a rectangular lace shawl with lace edging and no outside bound-off stitches.

MATERIALS

Land-o-Lace Krissy [80% wool, 20% silk; 1200 yds per 100g skein] shown in Bruno

1 set 32 in US5 [3.75 mm] circular needles
1 set 47 in US5 [3.75 mm] circular needles
Large-eyed, blunt needle
Stitch markers

GAUGE

19 sts and 40 rows = 4 in [10cm] in pattern, blocked

FINISHED (BLOCKED) SIZE

Width: 22 in [55 cm]
Height: 70 in [178 cm]

INSTRUCTIONS

CO 12 sts using a provisional cast-on
Work the bottom border chart 9 times, then work rows 1-2 of the left border chart.

Place a marker. Pick up and purl 90 stitches (one in each bump along the edge) plus 1 stitch at the end. Place marker. Purl the first 9 stitches from the provisional cast-on, and knit the last 2 stitches from the provisional cast-on.

At this point you should have 113 stitches on your needles. These consist of the 11 sts for the left border, 91 sts for the body of the shawl, and 11 sts for the right border — each section separated by the stitch-markers.

Start working on the main body of the shawl using Chart A.

All rows are charted. Odd rows are right-side rows and even rows are wrong-side rows. Note that all right-side charted rows are read from right to left. All wrong-side charted rows are read from left to right.
Continue with Chart B. Rows 79-118 should be repeated as many times as required to reach the desired length of the shawl.

EDGING

After row 218 on Chart C, with the right side of the stole facing you, work rows 1-20 of the top border. The green ∧ means that you knit that stitch together with a stitch on the main body. — means that you slip the first stitch on every even row.

BOTTOM BORDER

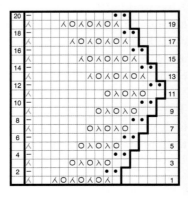

TOP BORDER

TOP BORDER CHART

When you have worked the top border 9 times, one stitch remains on the main body of the shawl. Work row 1 of the top border, joining it with the last stitch on the main body, and graft the top border to the left border.

Sew in the ends and block.

CHART LEGEND

Note that all rows are charted.
Note that all right-side (odd) charted rows are read from right to left.
All wrong-side (even) charted rows are read from left to right.
The 7 nupp-stitches are to be purled together on the subsequent WS-row.

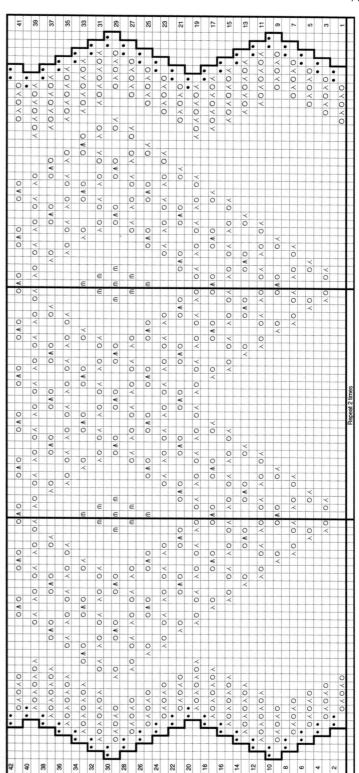

CHART A

78

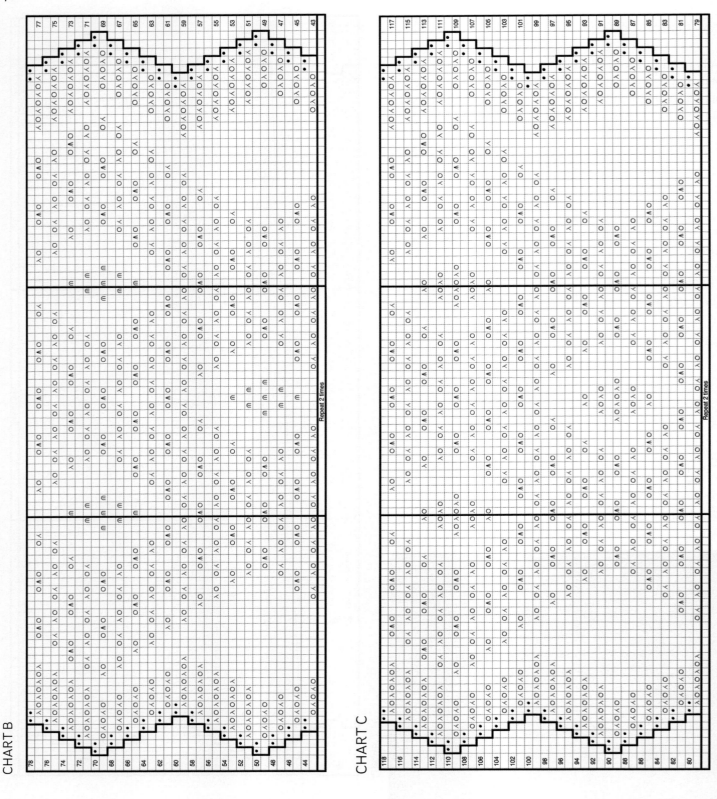

CHART B

CHART C

80

CHART D

CHART E

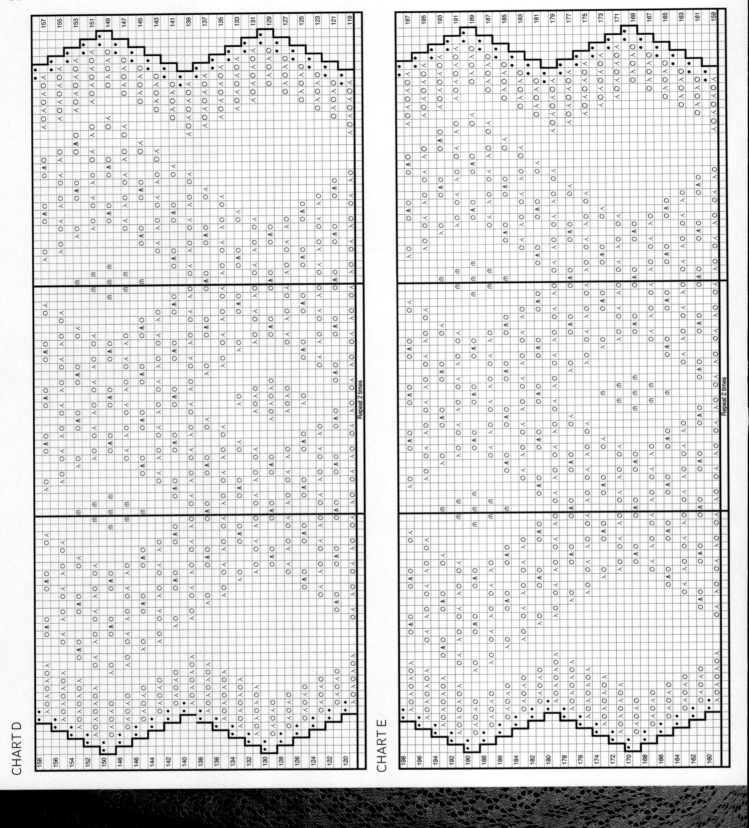

CHART F

Repeat 3 times

Chapter EIGHT:
Square Shawls

There are several different ways to knit a square shawl. Three main constructions come to mind:

+ straight square
+ corner to corner
+ center out

Designing a shawl as a straight square is really exactly the same as knitting a rectangular shawl as discussed in chapter 2; cast on however many stitches are required for the desired width, and then knit enough rows to make it a square. The lace motif will grow in the direction of the knitting, so if you would like to make your pattern symmetrical, keep in mind that the sides, beginning and end will all be outer edges.

It is also possible to design a square shawl from corner to corner. In that case, think of the square as two triangles. Cast on as for a bottom up triangle shawl (chapter 3) and increase one stitch at the beginning and one stitch at the end of every right side row. When the row is as wide as the diagonal of your desired size square, you start decreasing one stitch at the beginning and one stitch at the end of every right side row. With this type of construction the lace pattern will run diagonally on the square shawl.

This is a very good construction to use if you would like to maximize the usage of your yarn, and yet not run out of yarn at the end. Weigh the yarn prior to casting on. Note the weight, and then work a triangle, exactly like in chapter 3. then keep increasing on every right side row until you have used half of the yarn. It's a good idea to re-weigh the yarn when you reach reach the halfway point, just to be on the safe side. And maybe err slightly on the side of caution and leave an extra gram or two for the second half. Once the halfway point is reached, start decreasing on every right side row to work the second half of the square.

The third type of construction for a square shawl is to start in the center and knit outwards. This means that the shawl will be knit in the round. In this case, you are building four triangles. It is similar to how a neck-to-edge triangle shawl is constructed (chapter 4), just that in order to build a square shawl you make four triangles, and for a neck-to-edge triangular shawl you make two triangles. On every odd round the stitch count is increased by 8 stitches (two for each triangle).

When casting on, you need four stitches that are going to be designated the "corner stitches" — they are the square analogy to the "center stitch" or "spine" in the neck-to-edge triangular shawl. Each of these stitches will separate the triangles, and the increases will occur just before and just after each of these four stitches.

You also need stitches for the peak of the triangle pointing in towards the center of the shawl. I opted for one stitch per triangle = 4 stitches. So for Aranidae the total number of stitches cast on are 8.

Araneidae

The Araneidae lace shawl is named after the orb-weaver spider family. The orb weavers are the most common type of spiders that create the spiral shaped spider webs often seen in forests and gardens. The spider webs are delicate designs, built in the round, just like this type of square lace shawl.

MATERIALS

Rocky Mountain Dyeworks Mistaya Lace [100% merino; 960 yds per 90 g skein] 1.5 skein shown in Orb Weaver
1 32 inch US 5 [3.75 mm] circular needles
1 47 inch US 5 [3.75 mm] circular needles
1 set US 5 [3.75 mm] dpns
Large-eyed, blunt needle
Stitch markers

GAUGE

19 sts and 32 rows = 4 in [10 cm] in pattern, blocked

FINISHED (BLOCKED) SIZE

Width: 44 in [112 cm]
Height: 44 in [112 cm]

INSTRUCTIONS

CO 8 sts using invisible loop or other circular cast-on
Divide evenly on 4 dpns (switch to circular needles when you have enough stitches on the needles, and use magic loop)
Set up row 1: K8, place a marker so you can keep track of the beginning of each row
Setup row 2: (k, yo) 8 times - 16 sts
Set up row 3: K16
Set up row 4: [k, (yo, k3, yo)] 4 times - 24 sts
Set up row 5: K24

At this point you start knitting from the chart. All rows are charted.

All odd rounds are: [k, charted-row] 4 times
All even rounds are: [k, (yo, charted-row, yo)] 4 times

Chart A:

Work rounds 20-27 a total of 10 times. Each time these rounds are worked, add one repeat of the stitches in the box. Then continue with round 100 on chart B.

Work Chart C, then Chart D.

FINISHING INSTRUCTIONS

Round 131: Purl
Round 132: [K, (yo, k135, yo)] 4 times
Round 133: Purl

Then bind off as follows: K2, *return to left needle, k2tog through back loop, k1, repeat from * until no unworked stitches remain. Sew in ends and block.

When blocking, pull each double increase on row 129, as well as the four corner stitches to a point for the edging.

Note: the 7 nupp stitches should be knit together through the back loop on the subsequent row.

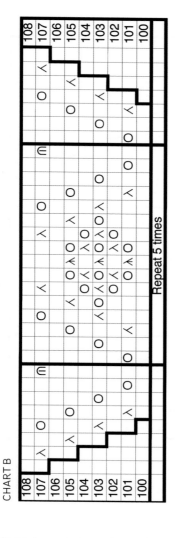

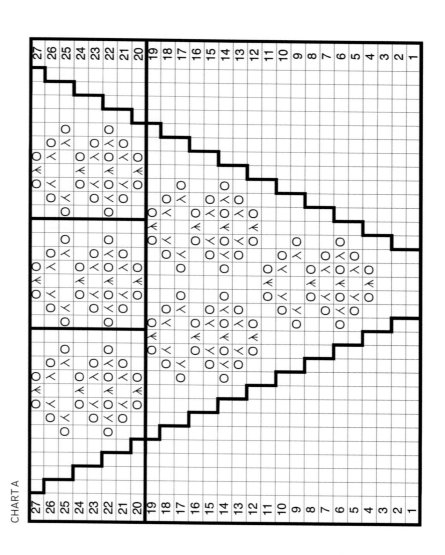

86

CHART C

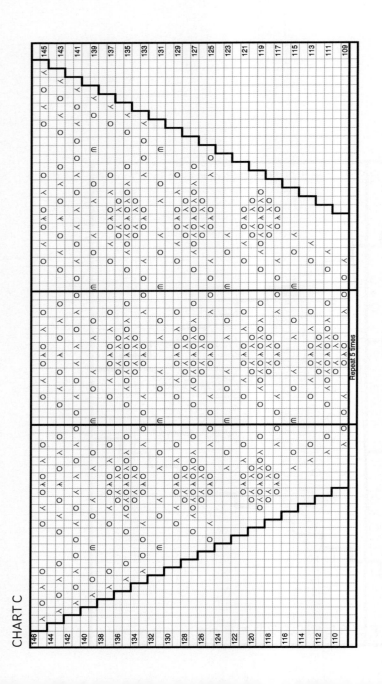

CHART D

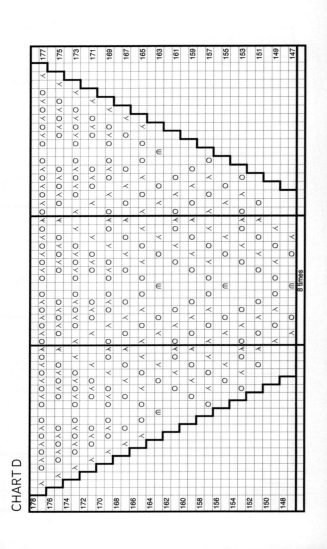

Mystic Air

CONSTRUCTION TECHNIQUES

Once these constructions have been mastered, it is of course possible to combine them for visual interest in a shawl. For example, Mystic Air is knit starting with a straight square that forms the center of the shawl. Once the center square is completed, pick up stitches around the square and continue working the raindrop section in the round. At this point the increases are done on every other row at the corners, very similar to the center-out construction. This change in the construction means that the raindrop section acts as a frame around the center section, and is perfectly symmetrical on all four sides.

The final part of the Mystic Air pattern is a knit-on border. Again the direction of the knitting changes, and the border is worked one small triangle at a time around the entire square shawl. All of these changes in knitting direction add to the visual interest of the shawl and allow the lace patterns to build in different ways.

This square shawl is part of the Mystic Elements series (following Mystic Waters, Mystic Light and Mystic Earth). The center portion of the shawl is light and airy, and then the borders surrounding it are filled with rain-drops as a reminder that clouds are made of water.

MATERIALS

2 skeins TriCoterie Alpaca Cashsilk [70% Baby Alpaca, 20% silk, 10% cashmere; 1312 yds per 100g skein] shown in Bella Swan
32 in length US 4 [3.5 mm] circular needles
47 or 60 in length US 4 [3.5 mm] circular needles
Large-eyed, blunt needle
Stitch markers

GAUGE

16 sts and 34 rows = 4 in [10 cm] in stockinette, blocked

FINISHED (BLOCKED) SIZE

There are three possible sizes for Mystic Air. The blocked dimensions of the various sizes are:

Large version (original) 63 in x 63 in [160 cm x 160 cm]
Medium version 55 in x 55 in [140 cm x 140 cm]
Small version 49 in x 49 in [124 cm x 124 cm]

INSTRUCTIONS

Center Section (all sizes):
CO 141 sts using a provisional cast-on
Row 1-3: K141
Row 4: K2, p137, k2
Work charts A-E.

Note: only right-side rows are charted. All wrong-side rows are: K2, p137, k2

90

CHART A1

| 69 | 67 | 65 | 63 | 61 | 59 | 57 | 55 | 53 | 51 | 49 | 47 | 45 | 43 | 41 | 39 | 37 | 35 | 33 | 31 | 29 | 27 | 25 | 23 | 21 | 19 | 17 | 15 | 13 | 11 | 9 | 7 | 5 | 3 | 1 |

CHART A2

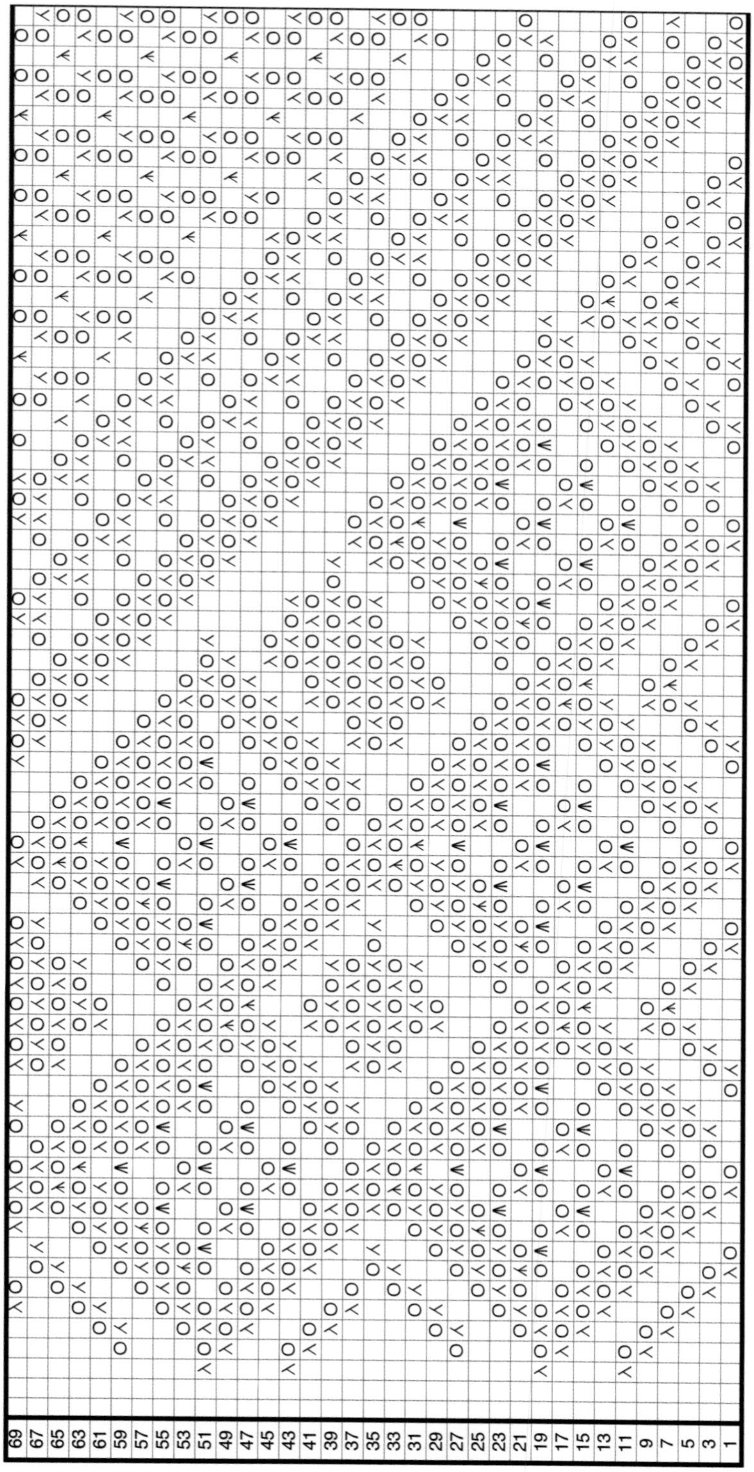

CHART B1

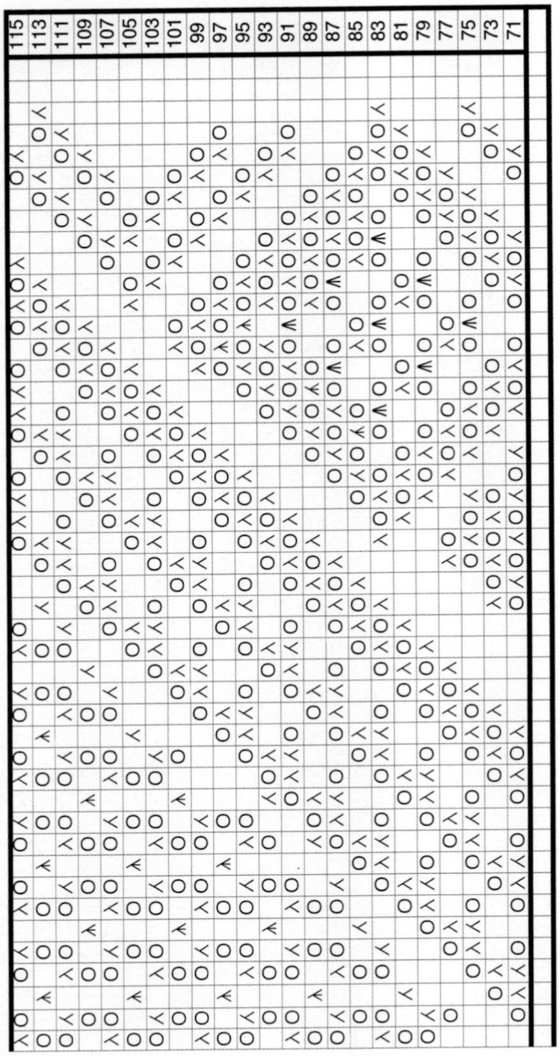

CHART B2

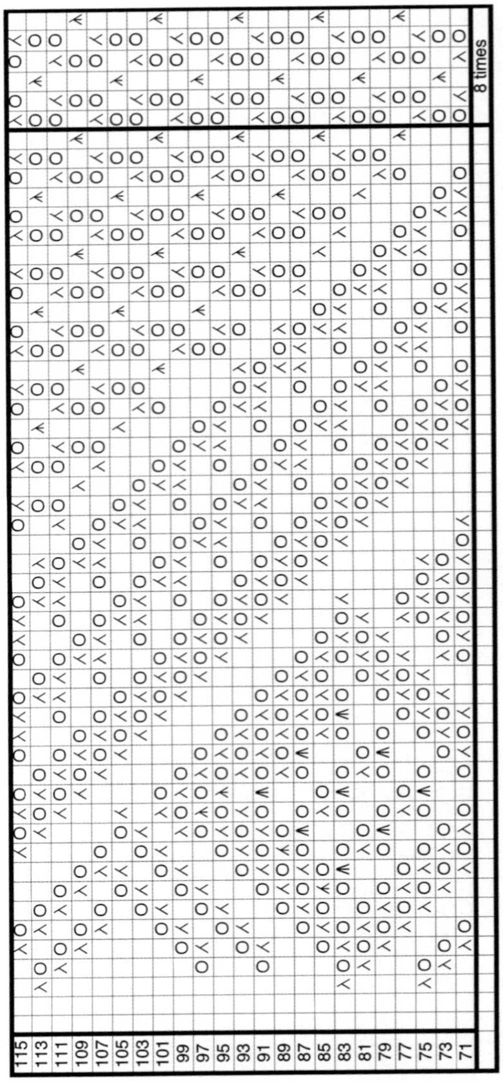

CHART C

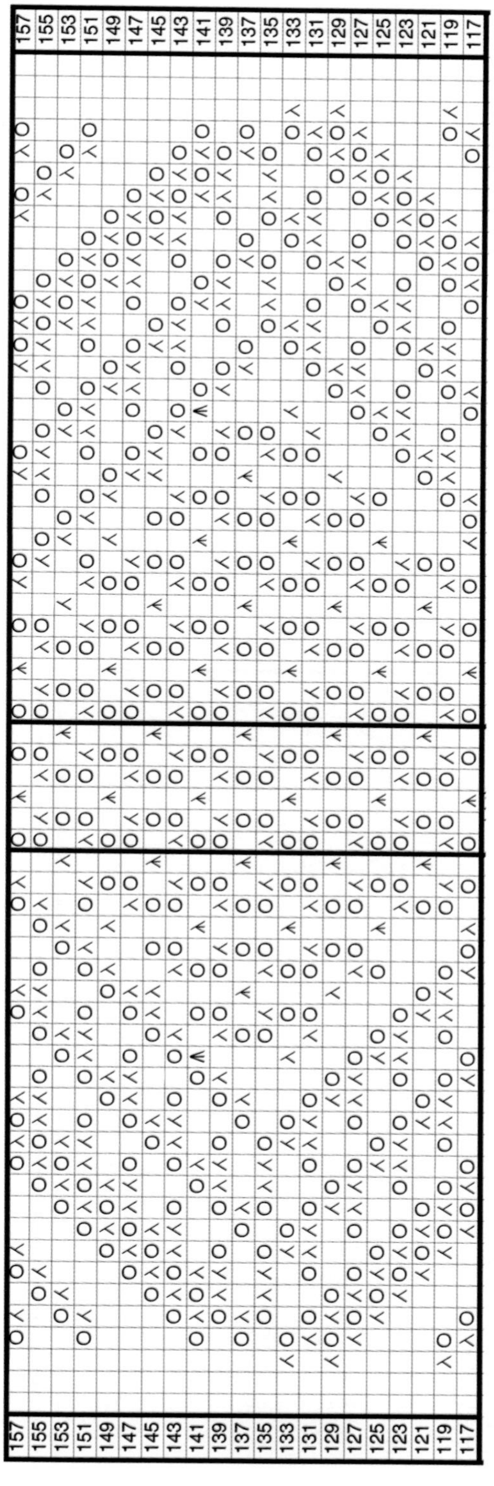

Column numbers (top): 157 155 153 151 149 147 145 143 141 139 137 135 133 131 129 127 125 123 121 119 117

Column numbers (bottom): 157 155 153 151 149 147 145 143 141 139 137 135 133 131 129 127 125 123 121 119 117

94

CHART D1

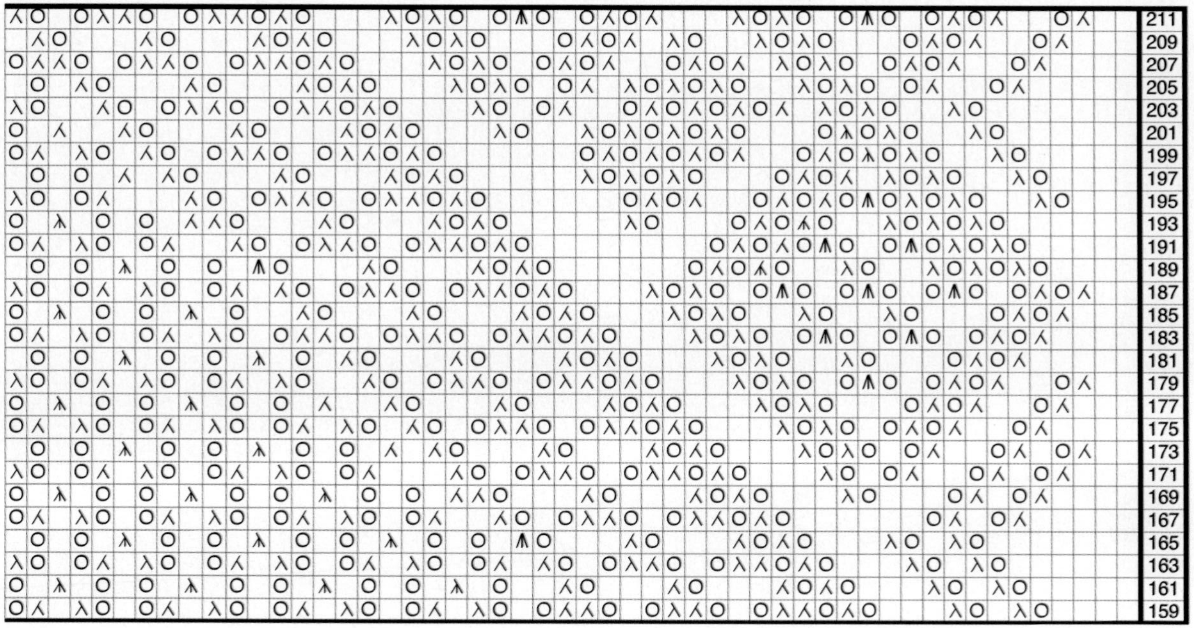

211 209 207 205 203 201 199 197 195 193 191 189 187 185 183 181 179 177 175 173 171 169 167 165 163 161 159

CHART D2

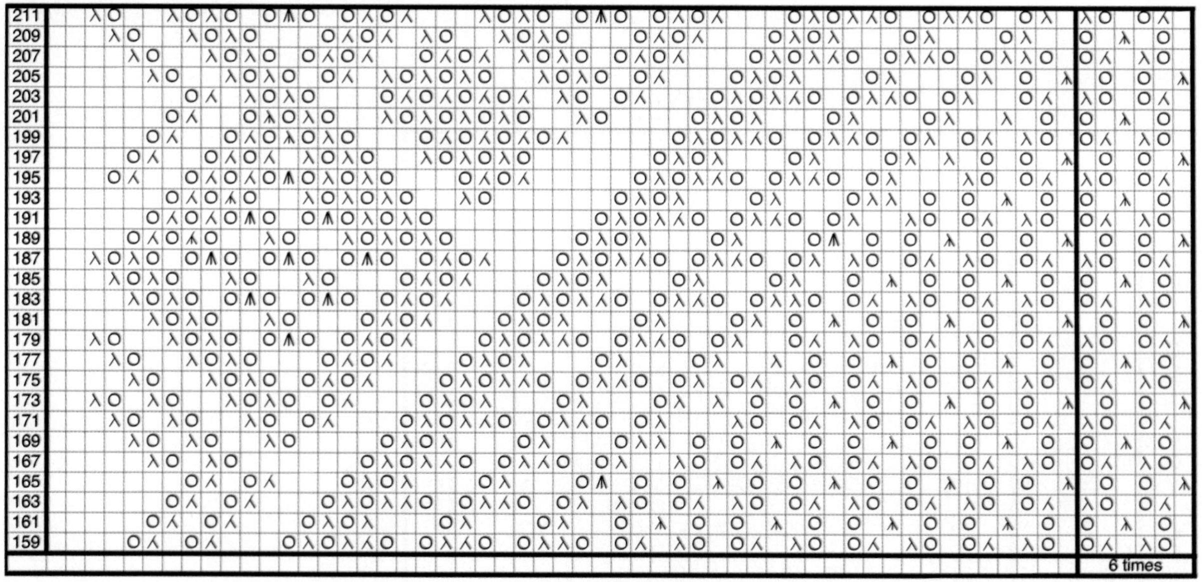

211 209 207 205 203 201 199 197 195 193 191 189 187 185 183 181 179 177 175 173 171 169 167 165 163 161 159

6 times

CHART E1

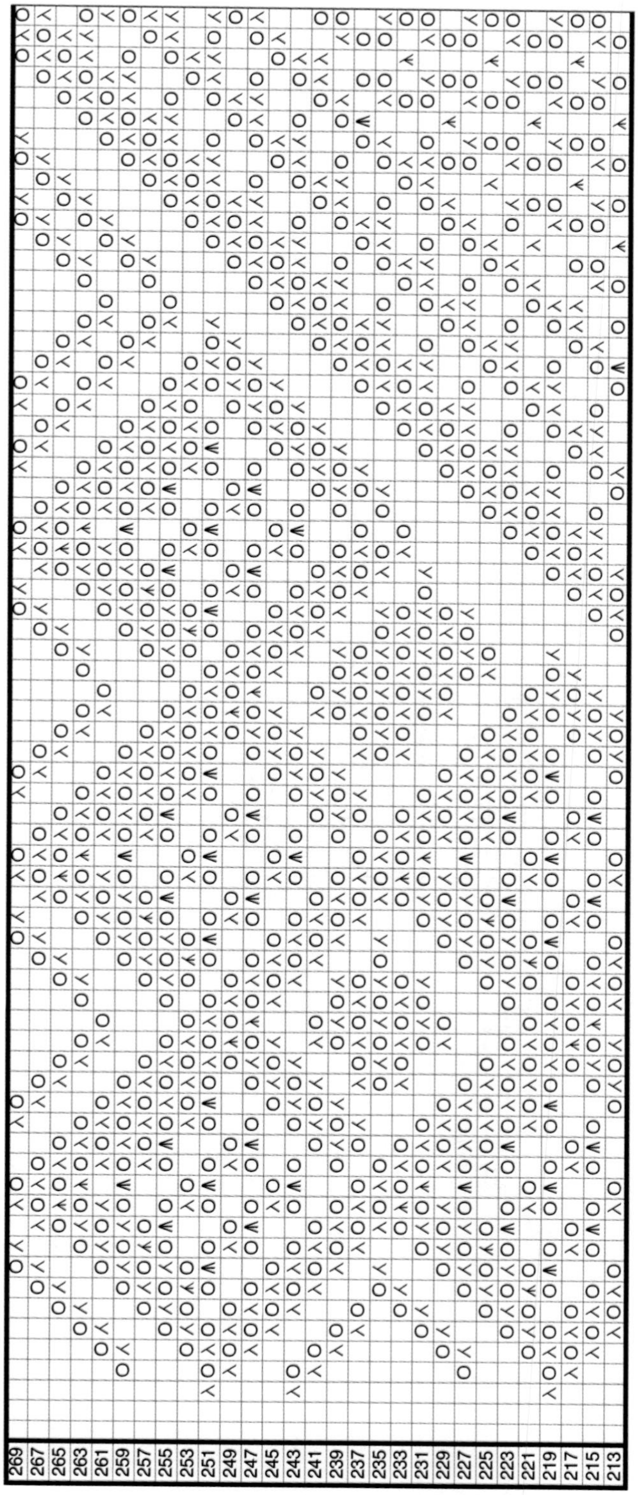

CHART E2

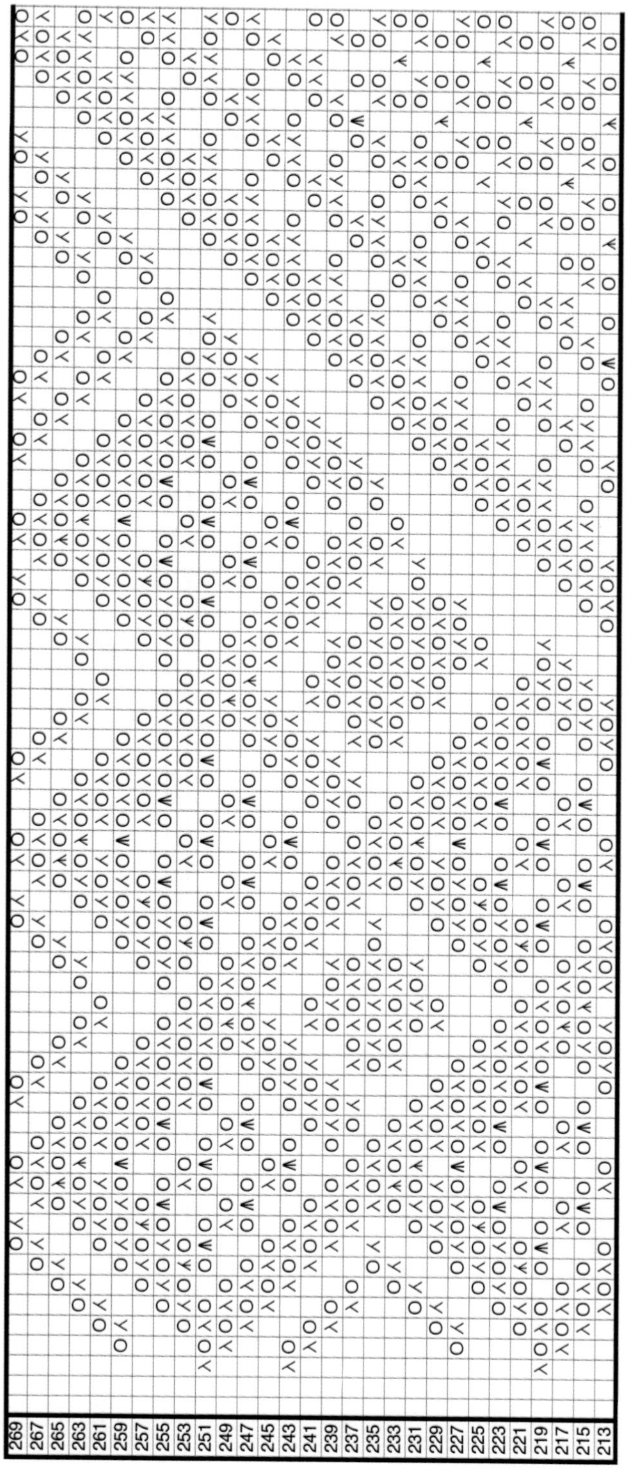

CHART F

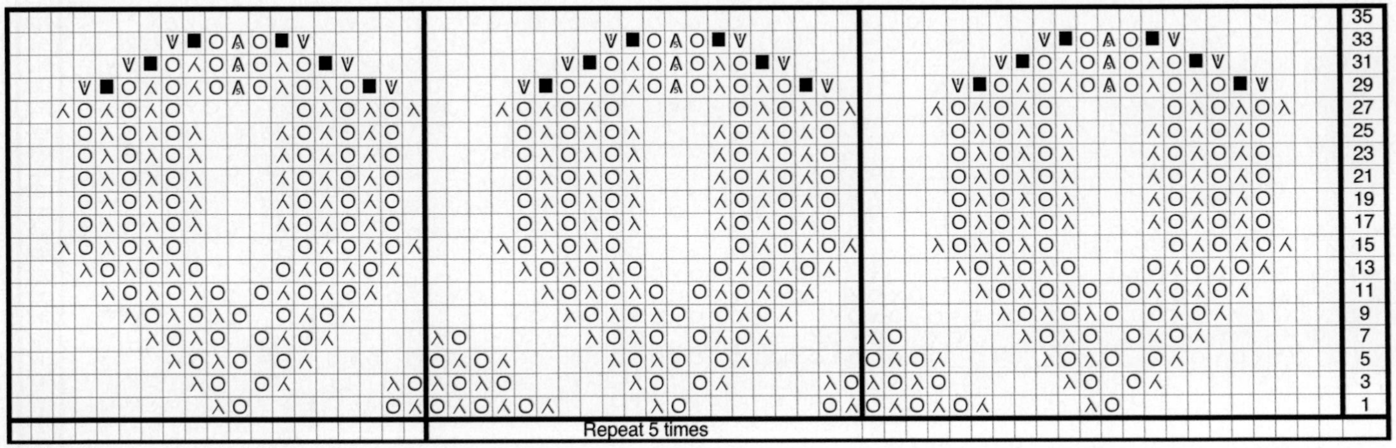

Repeat 5 times

CORNER CHART

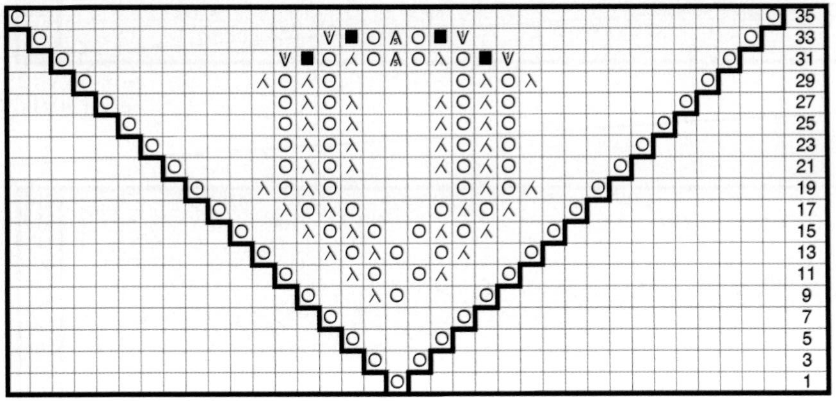

CHART G

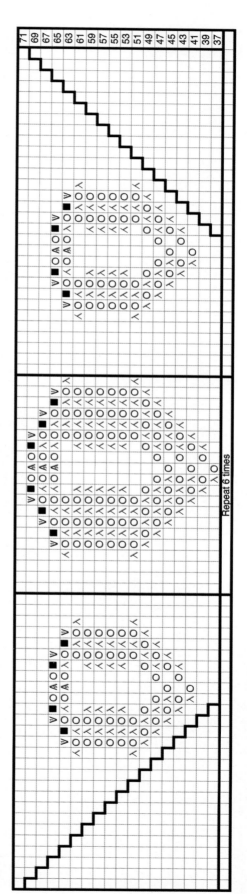

CORNER CHART 2

After row 269:
Row 270 (ws): K2, p137, k2
Row 271: K141
Row 272: K141 (***this is a good place to switch to a longer cord on your circular needles)
Row 273: K141, place marker. This spot will mark the beginning of your new rounds, so it is convenient if this marker is different from the other markers.

Pick up and knit 141 stitches along the left edge of the shawl. Place marker.
Pick up and knit 141 stitches along the cast-on edge. Place marker.
Pick up and knit 141 stitches along the right edge of the shawl. Place marker.
Knit 141 stitches along the top of the shawl. (Now you are back to the marker for the beginning of the new rounds).

Knit one full round (564 sts).

FIRST SET OF RAINDROPS (MEDIUM AND LARGE SIZE ONLY)

The next 36 rounds will be knit as follows:
Odd rounds: [corner-chart1, chart D] 4 times
Even rounds: knit all stitches

Corner Chart 1

Chart F

SECOND SET OF RAINDROPS (LARGE VERSION ONLY)

At this point, move the marker for the beginning of the rounds to be right after the column of YOs. The YO will continue to be the first stitch of the round. For the subsequent round, the YO will become the last stitch of the round.
The rounds 37-72 will be knit as follows:
Odd rounds: [corner-chart2, chart E] 4 times
Even rounds: knit all stitches

Corner Chart 2

Chart E

At this point you have 840 stitches on your needles. Break the yarn. Then cast on 14 stitches with a provisional cast-on.

Work row 17 of the edging-chart and attach the last stitch of row 17 to the first stitch in the round of the shawl. Continue with row 18-20 of the edging chart, attaching the edging to subsequent stitches in the last round knit on the square shawl (round 72).

EDGING

Continue using the edging chart, knit rows 1-20 and repeat 83 times. Then start an 84th repeat and knit up to and including row 15. Break the yarn and graft together with the cast-on side of the border starting at the main body of the shawl moving towards the outer edge. Sew in ends and block.

MEDIUM VERSION

Knit the center section as written, and the first set of raindrops.
At this point, move the marker for the beginning of the rounds to be right after the column of yos. The yo will continue to be the first stitch of the round.
For the subsequent round, the yo will become the last stitch of the round.

EDGING CHART 1

20	-						λ	O	λ	O	λ			•	•				19
18	-							λ	O	λ	O	λ		•	•				17
16	-				λ	O			λ	O	λ	O	λ	•	•				15
14	-			O	λ	O	λ		λ	O	λ	O	λ		•	•			13
12	-		λ	O	λ	O	λ	O				O	λ	O			•	•	11
10	-			O	λ	O	λ				O	λ	O			•	•		9
8	-				λ	O				O	λ	O			•	•			7
6	-					O	λ	O					•	•					5
4	-						O	λ	O				•	•					3
2	-					λ	O	λ	O	λ									1

Round 37: [yo, k33, yo, k143] 4 times - 712 sts
Round 38: knit all stitches
Round 39: [yo, k33, yo, k145] 4 times - 720 sts
Round 40: knit all stitches

At this point you should have 720 sts on your needles.
Break the yarn. Then cast on 14 stitches with a provisional cast-on.
Knit row 17 of the edging-chart and attach the last stitch of row 17 to the first stitch in the round of the shawl. Continue with row 18-20 of the edging chart, attaching the edging to subsequent stitches in the last round knit on the square shawl.
Continue using the edging chart, knit rows 1-20 and repeat 83 times.
Then start an 84th repeat and knit up to and including row 15.
Break the yarn and graft together with the cast-on side of the border starting at the main body of the shawl moving towards the outer edge.
Sew in ends and block.

SMALL VERSION

Knit the center section as written, including the instructions to pick up the stitches along the sides, place markers and knit one full round of 564 sts). After that, do NOT knit any of the raindrops.
Instead, knit the next 10 rows as follows:
Round 1: [yo, k141] 4 times
Round 2: knit all stitches
Round 3: [yo, k1, yo, k141] 4 times
Round 4: knit all stitches
Round 5: [yo, k3, yo, k141] 4 times
Round 6: knit all stitches
Round 7: [yo, k5, yo, k141] 4 times
Round 8: knit all stitches
Round 9: [yo, k7, yo, k141] 4 times
Round 10: knit all stitches

At this point you should have 600 sts on your needles.
Break the yarn. Then cast on 12 stitches with a provisional cast-on.
Knit row 5 of the edging-chart and attach the last stitch of row 5 to the first stitch in the round of the shawl. Continue with row 6-20 of the edging chart, attaching the edging to subsequent stitches in the last round knit on the square shawl.
Continue using the edging chart, knit rows 1-20 and repeat 59 times. On the 60th repeat you will only knit rows 1-5. Break the yarn and graft together with the cast-on side of the border starting at the main body of the shawl moving towards the outer edge.
Sew in ends and block.

The Mystic Air construction is probably the most complicated one in the book, simply because it combines a number of techniques. But it serves as a good example of the fact that these techniques don't have to be used in isolation, but rather as a starting point to come up with more complex designs. For example, combining a bottom-up triangle with a rectangular stole can result in a stole with pointed ends. And using the strategy for knitting borders with a rectangular shawl but applying it to a triangular shawl can result in a triangular shawls with borders knit with the shawl. The possibilities are endless, and it is my sincere hope that you will use these constructions described in this book to create your own unique designs.

Abbreviations

BO — bind off

CO — cast on

k — knit

kfb — knit in the front and then in the back of the same stitch

ktbl — knit through the back loop

k2tog — knit 2 stitches together

k3tog — knit 3 stitches together

k4tog — knit 4 stitches together

ln — left needle

M1 — make 1 stitch by picking up the strand between the two stitches and ktbl

nupp — [k1, yo] 3 times, k all into the same stitch

p — purl

PM — place marker

psso — pass slipped stitch(es) over

p2tog — purl 2 stitches together

rn — right needle

rs — right side

sl — slip

sl1 — slip 1 stitch

ssk — slip stitch as if to knit, slip stitch as if to knit, replace on left needle and knit both stitches together through the back loop

ssp — slip stitch as if to knit, slip stitch as if to knit, replace on left needle and purl both stitches together through the back loop

st, sts — stitch(es)

yo — yarn over

ws — wrong side

w5 — work 5 stitches together as follows: ssk, k3tog, pass previous stitch (the one from the ssk) over

Stitch Legend

BASIC STITCHES

□ – k on right side, p on wrong side
• – p on right side, k on wrong side
Ҩ – ktbl
− – sl1
■ – stitch does not exist

INCREASES

O – yarn over
V – kfb

DECREASES

ᴧ – k2tog on right side
λ – ssk on right side, k2tog on wrong side
Ѧ – slip 2 stitches together (knitwise), knit 1 stitch, pass slipped stitches over
ᴧ̇ – k3tog
⨺ – k4tog
λ̇ – sl 1, k2tog, psso
⨹ – sl1, k3tog, psso

CABLE STITCHES

Ƴ–ᴧ – slip 2 stitches onto a cable needle and hold behind the work, knit 1 stitch off the left hand needle, replace the leftmost stitch from the cable needle onto the left needle and knit that stitch, then knit the stitch off the cable needle

λ–ᴟ – slip 2 stitches onto a cable needle and hold in front of the work, knit 1 stitch off the left hand needle, replace the leftmost stitch from the cable needle onto the left needle and knit that stitch, then knit the stitch off the cable needle

Ƴᴧ – slip 1 stitch onto cable needle, hold behind the work, k1 off left needle, k1 off cable needle

ᴟᴟ – slip 1 stitch onto cable needle, hold in front of work, k1 off left needle, k1 off cable needle

SPECIAL STITCHES

3x3 – make 3 from 3 by k3tog-yo-k into same stitch
Ⅲ – work 3 sts as follows: insert rn into 3rd stitch on ln and pass over previous 2 sts, then k, yo, k
Ѧ – work 5 stitches together as follows: ssk, k3tog, pass previous stitch (the one from the ssk) over
Ⴖ – nupp: [k1, yo] 3 times, k all into the same stitch

PATTERN SPECIFIC-LEGENDS

Remember, the legend for Changing Directions is different as it is worked in garter stitch:

□ – k on rs and ws
ᴧ – k2tog on rs
λ – ssk on rs
⨺ – k2tog on ws
⨹ – ssk on ws
ᴧ̇ – k3tog on rs
⨹ – k3tog on ws
Ѧ – sl2 sts together, knitwise, k, pssso
O – yo
Ҩ – ktbl

Recommended Books

There are a number of stitch dictionaries that can be helpful when designing a lace shawl. A few suggestions include:

- *A Treasury of Knitting Patterns* (volumes 1-4), by Barbara G Walker (Schoolhouse Press, 1998/2000)
- *Vogue Knitting Stitchionary Volume Five: Lace Knitting* (Sixth & Spring Books, 2010)
- *Omas Strickgeheimnisse* by Erika Eichenseer, Erika Grill and Betta Kron (Rosenheimer Verlagshaus, 2000)
- *The Haapsalu Shawl: A Knitted Lace Tradition from Estonia* by Siiri Reimann and Aime Edasi (Search Press Ltd 2011)
- *Gossamer Webs: The History and Techniques of Orenburg Lace Shawls* by Galina Khmeleva (Interweave Press, 1998)
- Japanese Stitch Dictionaries, e.g. *Knitting Patterns Book 250* by Hitomi Shida and *Knitting Patterns 300 Lace*

Acknowledgements

Alison Holley of Vancouver has been my trusted test-knitter for years, and for this book she both test-knit and was a sample knitter for 2 of the shawls.

Yarn was graciously supplied by Handmaiden, Land O Lace, Rocky Mountain Dyeworks, Slackford Studio, Spirit Trail Fiberworks, SweetGeorgia, Tri'Coterie and Zen Yarn Garden.

Yarns appearing in the book include:

Perilla: Cashsilk from SweetGeorgia in Boysenberry – chapter 2
Margarita Leaves: Serenity Silk from Zen Garden in Margarita – chapter 3
Magic Lanterns: Nona from Spirit Trail Fiberworks – chapter 4
Mystic Roses: Lace-Garn from Wollmeise in Rosenrot – chapter 5
Tidal Waves: Swiss Mountain Sea Sock from Handmaiden in Topaz – chapter 6
Changing Directions: Glacier Lace from Rocky Mountain Dyeworks in Calendula – chapter 6
Chandelier Shawl: Nimbus Cloud from Slackford Studios in True Blood – chapter 6
Blueberry Patch: Krissy from Land-O-Lace in Bruno – chapter 7
Araneidae: Mistaya Lace from Rocky Mountain Dyeworks in Orb Weaver – chapter 8
Mystic Air: Alpaca Cashsilk from Tri'Coterie in Bella Swan – chapter 8

About Anna Dalvi

Anna Dalvi has been publishing knitting patterns on-line since 2007. She has self published 50+ patterns over the past several years. Her most popular designs are the Mystic lace shawls, published in a mystery knitalong format, which have attracted 5,000+ knitters worldwide. She is also the designer behind the popular Seasons of Lace series. Her website has had 75,000 readers in the past year, and the readership grows annually. In her knitting, Anna enjoys variety more than anything else — from intricate lace to sprawling cables, and differences in color and texture.

Anna holds a B.S. in Computer Science from Cornell University, and an M.B.A. from Queens University.

knitandknag.com

About Cooperative Press

partners in publishing

Cooperative Press (*formerly anezka media*) was founded in 2007 by Shannon Okey, a voracious reader as well as writer and editor, who had been doing freelance acquisitions work, introducing authors with projects she believed in to editors at various publishers.

Although working with traditional publishers can be very rewarding, there are some books that fly under their radar. They're too avant–garde, or the marketing department doesn't know how to sell them, or they don't think they'll sell 50,000 copies in a year.

5,000 or 50,000. Does the book matter to that 5,000? Then it should be published.

In 2009, Cooperative Press changed its named to reflect the relationships we have developed with authors working on books. We work together to put out the best quality books we can and share in the proceeds accordingly.

Thank you for supporting independent publishers and authors.

cooperativepress.com

Also by Cooperative Press

+ *Purls Forever,* Jonelle Raffino
+ *The Knitgrrl Guide to Professional Knitwear Design,* Shannon Okey
+ *Silk Road Socks,* Hunter Hammersen
+ *What Would Madame Defarge Knit?,* Heather Ordover

Coming soon

+ *Extreme Double Knitting,* Alasdair Post-Quinn
+ *Beyond Knit & Purl,* Kate Atherley
· *Big Foot Knits,* Andi Smith

Sample Charts

Create your own designs using these chart samples. You may wish to print or copy them and enlarge when you first begin working.

SAMPLE SQUARE

SAMPLE BOTTOM-UP TRIANGLE

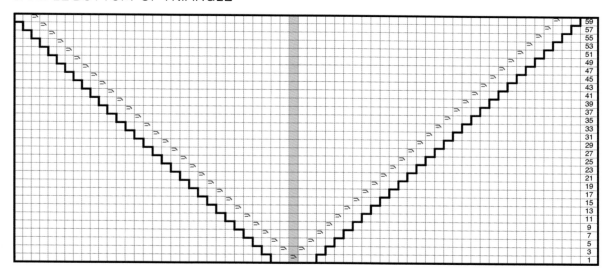

SAMPLE NECK-TO-EDGE TRIANGLE

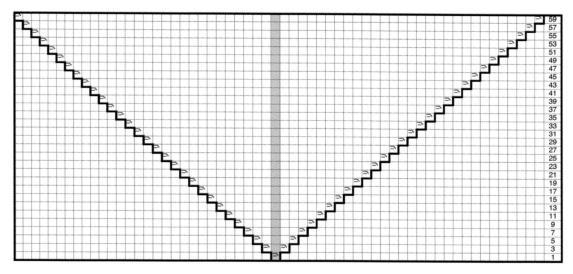

CRAFTS/KNITTING

Anna Dalvi of Knit & Knag Designs brings both her design sensibility and logical mind to bear in this book for new and experienced lace knitters alike. Ten different shawls are divided into chapters based on shaping and construction techniques, teaching concepts in a fresh new way. You'll use not only diagrams and charts but also mathematical means of keeping your designs in line. Ever wonder why your stitch count is off on another pattern? Anna will show you what deltas are, how they work, and much more in this extraordinary book.

Join Anna Dalvi for a shawl-design-seminar-in-a-book that keeps light bulbs going off while making the material seem simple. Her genius lies in boiling down tricky concepts to their essence and presenting them in a warm, practical style. Anna's own inspiring patterns not only accompany, but illustrate the design techniques throughout. Using Shaping Shawls, knitters will be able to create shawls in any shape for any occasion with confidence.

—Jaala Spiro, KnitCircus magazine, knitcircus.com

With a lucidness of style that is almost magical, Anna manages to take an apparently opaquely complex subject and make it seem so simple that you think something must be missing. The way she describes lace shawl design is so clear that you'll walk away with the confidence that you can design a dozen of them immediately yourself, even if you are just a beginning lace knitter. This book is definitely going into my knitting library!

—Gryphon Perkins, the Sanguine Gryphon, sanguinegryphon.com

Anna explains lace patterns in a detailed and intricate way, but her methodology is incredibly clear at the same time. These breathtaking designs will appeal to lace knitters of many different levels.

—Ragga Eiriksdottir, Knitting Iceland, knittingiceland.is

COOPERATIVE PRESS
partners in publishing

ISBN 978-0-9792017-6-9

52695

9 780979 201769